Praise for
Beautiful Resistance

"I believe Jon is one of the great prolific and prophetic voices of our generation. He's been a pastor in my life for over a decade, starting with my years in New York. Jon casts a timely and compelling vision in his latest work, *Beautiful Resistance*. He writes with such astute analysis and poignant clarity that several times throughout these pages, I wanted to stand and shout, 'I'm in!' May these words be a clarion call to the church to fortify our faith through sacrifice and love."

—REBEKAH LYONS,
bestselling author of *Rhythms of Renewal* and *You Are Free*

"Western culture is increasingly hostile to the teachings and ways of Jesus. The pressure to compromise is the highest it's been in my lifetime. The urge to back down on Jesus's compelling vision of life in the kingdom is greater than ever. This book comes at just the right time—a pastoral, yet prophetic call from one of our generation's greatest leaders. I was moved in my heart to trust Jesus's vision of life over that of my culture's."

—JOHN MARK COMER, author of *The Ruthless Elimination of Hurry*

"It's one thing to write on the beauties of the kingdom and how the way of Jesus must be esteemed as better and stronger than the kingdom of this world; it's another thing altogether to live this. Jon Tyson lives this. He writes and preaches with a uniquely compelling conviction, because it flows from a figure that truly believes that the words and ways of Jesus are better than all this world has to offer. By the end of this book, you will find yourself compelled to join with the likes of Dietrich Bonhoeffer who knew that the beauties of the kingdom of heaven are better than the allure of this world."

—DR. BRYAN LORITTS, author of *The Dad Difference*

"Jon challenges us to boldly live without compromise, and he gives us the practical tools to do it. This book is incisive, challenging, and daring. It will stay with you."

—Scott Harrison, founder of charity: water, and author of *Thirst*

"I have witnessed Jon live out this unflinching message in the heart of New York City while he leads a thriving community, disciples his children, and inspires the church around the world to radically commit to the gospel. Few people stir my spirit to the depths that Jon does. Whether it's sitting across the table at a diner talking with him about all God is doing, reading something he has written, or hearing one of his sermons, my heart is awakened once again to the radical call to follow Jesus, no matter the cost. The message found in the pages of *Beautiful Resistance* is one needed at this very hour. In a way that only Jon Tyson can, with such brilliance and eloquence, he paints a picture of what the true disciple's life looks like in a culture that is longing to see the beauty of Jesus manifested in the lives of his followers."

—Banning Liebscher,
founder and pastor of Jesus Culture and author of *Rooted*

"*Beautiful Resistance* is one of the most compelling and defiant books I've read in a long time. I love Jon's radical, no-messing vision of the church as a prophetic community. This is a wake-up call for us all from the heart of a man who lives his message, loves his city, and serves his Lord with a passion and intelligence destined to become less rare."

—Pete Greig, founder of the 24-7 Prayer movement

"In every generation, the church is called to resist powerful spiritual and cultural forces that wreak havoc in our lives and communities. Sadly, the depth of life that makes resistance possible often goes missing, resulting in our ongoing capitulation to various powers. But it doesn't have to be this way. Jon Tyson offers us a compelling vision of resistance. It's one marked not by fear but by joy. I'm grateful for this wonderful resource."

—RICH VILLODAS, lead pastor of New Life Fellowship

"We can see that the body of Christ has thrived and struggled throughout various seasons over the centuries. We are currently in a moment in which all areas of our lives have been or are being redefined in front of our very eyes. It's quite polarizing, and in some ways it has caught us off guard. In *Beautiful Resistance*, Jon Tyson does a brilliant job of contextualizing the day we live in and giving us a clear path forward. The words, truth, and ideas in this book allow us to take a step back and better understand the days we live in, not just to observe it all but rather to engage in a way that mirrors the ways of Jesus. I know this book will give you a way forward and tactics to thrive in this time."

—ERIC JOHNSON, pastor of Bethel Church, speaker, and author

"In each age the church faces a challenge in which she is called to live out her heavenly call among the thorns and thickets of compromise and coercion. In *Beautiful Resistance*, Jon Tyson flips the challenges the church faces on their heads, showing us Jesus's better way and offering a hopeful vision of a church of conviction in an age of comprise."

—MARK SAYERS, senior pastor of Red Church and
    author of *Facing Leviathan* and *Reappearing Church*

Beautiful
RESISTANCE

THE JOY OF CONVICTION IN
A CULTURE OF COMPROMISE

JON TYSON

AUTHOR OF *THE BURDEN IS LIGHT*

MULTNOMAH

Library of Congress Cataloging-in-Publication Data
Names: Tyson, Jon, author.
Title: Beautiful resistance : the joy of conviction in a culture of compromise / Jon Tyson.
Description: First edition. | Colorado Springs, CO : Multnomah, 2020. | Includes bibliographical references.
Identifiers: LCCN 2019044494 | ISBN 9780735290693 (trade paperback) | ISBN 9780735290709 (ebook)
Subjects: LCSH: Christianity and culture. | Compromise (Ethics)
Classification: LCC BR115.C8 T97 2020 | DDC 261—dc23
LC record available at https://lccn.loc.gov/2019044494

Printed in the United States of America on acid-free paper

waterbrookmultnomah.com

2 4 6 8 9 7 5 3 1

First Edition

For Diane Cobb,
whose deep love and sacrificial care showed me that the
church could be a thing of staggering beauty.

His intent was that now, through the church, the manifold wisdom of God should be made known to the rulers and authorities in the heavenly realms.

EPHESIANS 3:10

CONTENTS

Introduction

I t's early in the morning and I am drinking bad coffee, trying to keep my eyes open after a late-night drive. I am in Poland, where I do not speak the language, cannot understand the street signs, and do not know exactly where I am going. I am trying to find a scene from the life of Dietrich Bonhoeffer that has haunted me since I read about it five years ago.

I drive along the Eastern Oder River. The air is warm; the day is quiet—not much in sight. There are no historical markers, no signs of what I am looking for.

Finally I see it—a small hill above the banks of the river. I park and walk up. From a clearing, as I knew I would, I have views down the river toward a place called Finkenwalde and up the hill to the site of a former German airfield. Here on this hill, eighty years earlier, a conversation took place that still resonates for me and for all who are concerned with whether Christ or culture will have the ascendancy in our generation.

A PLACE CALLED FINKENWALDE

Dietrich Bonhoeffer was one of Jesus's exemplary disciples of the last century. His faithfulness to Christ in the midst of a failing church has borne witness long after his short life. Bonhoeffer was not raised in a fundamentally religious home, yet exposure to the Roman Catholic Church during his travels, and relationships with some key Protestant theologians of his day, drew his heart into the beauty and power of the church. After completing his doctorate at the age of twenty-one, he grew to become a significant figure in the resistance against Hitler and the broken German church.

In 1933, the threat of Nazi power was growing in Germany and many were concerned about the compromise of the church with the Nazi movement. The church was capitulating to and cooperating with the Reich, handing the loyalties that belong to Christ to the Führer. Bonhoeffer expert Gaylon Barker pointed out, "Hitler did not merely want to rule Germany politically; rather, he wanted to control the hearts and souls of its citizens. At a very fundamental level, therefore, this was as much a religious battle as it was a political struggle."[1] It would eventually lead to one of the darkest moments in the history of the church and the extermination of more than six million Jews.

As many sat by, the takeover of the church accelerated. When a Nazi-supported group gained control of the German Evangelical Church, they wanted to exclude all non-Aryan clergy, revise the liturgy to make it more German, and even remove the Old Testament from the Bible. At a 1934 synod that led to the establishment of the Confessing Church, Bonhoeffer signed the Barmen Declaration, which was to become a manifesto of fidelity to Christ. Penned largely by Karl Barth, it declared the church was to be loyal to Christ and not to be an organ of the state.

Seeing the weakness of many German pastors and their lack of preparation for obedience to Christ and resistance to the regime, the Confessing Church sensed the need for stronger training. In 1935 Bonhoeffer accepted the invitation to create an underground seminary that would match orthodox belief with orthodox praxis. His vision was an intentional Christian community committed to living the ethic of Jesus found in the Sermon on the Mount.

In the providence of God, a large, empty house—originally a manor house of the von Katte family—was available near Stettin, in the rural town of Finkenwalde. There a schedule of study and common life began. Seminary life centered on prayer, the Scriptures, confession, and shared rhythms, and much of the vision was included in Bonhoeffer's well-known works *Life Together* and *The Cost of Discipleship*.

For the students, in the middle of the onslaught of hell, this was a portal to heaven. Bonhoeffer wrote during this period, "The physical presence of other Christians is a source of incomparable joy and strength to the believer."[2] Their daily rhythm of life together was built on a vision for a new kind of disciple, one characterized by fidelity to Jesus Christ despite the cost, one who believed in Christ's millennial reign, not that of the Reich. This robust vision of discipleship would be tested as the Gestapo would arrest more than two dozen Finkenwalde students after the seminary was shut down.

THIS MUST BE STRONGER THAN THAT

When Bonhoeffer's friends began to read copies of his sermons and hear reports about the intensity of the discipleship at Finkenwalde, questions began to arise. Was this level of formation truly necessary? Would the Finkenwalders burn out? Would they lose credibility and be seen as too extreme by the national leadership?

One friend in particular, a young historian named Wilhelm Niesel, who had heard Bonhoeffer lecture in 1933, came up from Berlin to visit, being "suspicious of too much 'spiritualism.'"[3] Bonhoeffer took Niesel on a rowing trip to the Oder Sound. One author described the scene this way:

> When the two rowers reached the far shore, Bonhoeffer led Niesel up a small hill to a clearing from which they could see in the distance a vast field and the "runways of a nearby squadron." German fighter planes were taking off and landing, and soldiers moved hurriedly in purposeful patterns, like so many ants. Bonhoeffer spoke of a new generation of Germans in training, whose disciplines were formed "for a kingdom . . . of hardness and cruelty." It would be necessary, he explained, to propose a superior discipline if the Nazis were to be defeated.

"You have to be stronger than these tormentors that you find
everywhere today."[4]

This image is the one that haunted me and drew me to the banks of the
Oder after a sleepless night of driving. Bonhoeffer, a pastor with unflinching
loyalty to the Cross, standing as a prophetic sign to the world. On the side of a
river, overlooking the massing Nazi troops, he stood in the shadow of eternity.
A man of convictions, a man of contrasts.

What he was doing in Finkenwalde had to be stronger than what Hitler
was doing with his army.

Discipleship must be stronger than cultural formation.

Loyalty must be stronger than compromise.

This must be stronger than that.

The times called for a beautiful resistance.

Such a prophetic stance was in some ways laughable. Bonhoeffer's seminary was small and its season short. The Gestapo would close the seminary in
1937. In many ways it was a feeble joke compared with the power of the Third
Reich.

But it was a prophetic seed of a faithful church. And over time, as Jesus
promised, that small seed grew and bore fruit. Today the Reich is a shameful
memory, Hitler is in the grave, and the German church is repentant. But the
fruit of Finkenwalde—the community, the vision, and the work—has gone on
to shape a vision of Christian discipleship that has inspired millions.

Bonhoeffer was right. This *must* be stronger than that. This *was* stronger
than that.

All this was running through my mind as I stood overlooking the Oder
Sound—perhaps at the very spot where Bonhoeffer once took his friend—
thinking about *our* cultural moment and the compromise rampant in our day.
*Should we just give up and capitulate to the powers of our time? Should we sit
by while our faith is taken captive by political and ideological forces? Should we
avert our eyes while mammon wreaks havoc on our hearts? Should we watch*

twenty million young people leave the church in our generation? A million a year give up on faith?[5] *Is it possible to build community in such a way that though it is small, generations to come will look back on our faithfulness in a generation of compromise?*

THE NEW RESISTANCE

I believe that what was true in the 1930s is true now. We live in a time when the church is compromising with the culture left, right, and center, and we're losing our influence. Though there is no specific "Hitler" pressuring us, we face a myriad of forces seeking to sabotage our faith. Because of the tectonic shift in sexuality, ethics, technology, secular ideologies, religion, and globalization, much of the familiar landscape has been swept away. In many areas our culture is almost unrecognizable compared with a generation ago. The spiritual devastation from much of this cultural change and the failure of the church to respond well have been almost unthinkable.

So we must call our generation to loyalty to Christ. We must live with devotion and conviction regardless of what they cost us. This must be stronger than that.

I am sure that you, too, have felt this conflict between the potential of the church and its compromise in our day, and I am sure that you have felt the conflict in your soul between who you are and whom God calls you to be. I'm speaking to you as a fellow disciple with urgency in my heart: this is the time for *our* beautiful resistance.

Chapter 1

A Church Coming Back to Life

[The church] exists ... to set up in the world a new sign which is radically dissimilar to [the world's] own manner and which contradicts it in a way which is full of promise.

KARL BARTH, *Church Dogmatics*

I will build my church.

Matthew 16:18

In a *New York Times* article entitled "Googling for God," Seth Stephens-Davidowitz wrote, "It has been a bad decade for God, at least so far."

Searches questioning God's existence are up. . . . Porn searches are up 83 percent. For heroin, it's 32 percent.

How are the Ten Commandments doing? Not well. "Love thy neighbor" is the most common search with the word "neighbor" in it, but right behind at No. 2 is "neighbor porn." The top Google search including the word "God" is "God of War," a video game.[1]

It's been a tough decade for God, and his church has not fared well either. The church that Jesus founded on his compassion and grace has at times failed to even resemble its founder. Celebrity pastor scandals; abuses in the

Catholic Church; political hijacking; indifference to the humanitarian crises of our day, including refugees, racism, and environmentalism; materialism; and complacency have caused many to leave the church.

I carry some cultural shame in this moment as a pastor. When I meet people and they ask what I do, I fumble for how to respond. I used to say witty and impressive things like "I am a consultant that specializes in helping the largest nonprofit on earth be more effective at caring for the poor and alleviating human suffering." Now I just tell them I am a pastor, and they often reply with a strained "Oh" and shuffle off to a less awkward conversation. I've sat over coffee with countless people—some of whom until recently were parishioners of mine—who say they cannot continue to be associated with Christianity after some of the things they have seen Christians say and do. I've *seen* and *felt* the change in the church's reputation. And I've been embarrassed by my fellow Christians' behavior more than once.

Yet no matter our disgust at the church's failure, Christ himself must feel the most grief. How can a community founded on enemy love be guilty of such distortions? Nietzsche once said, "Better songs they would have to sing to make me believe in their Redeemer: more redeemed would his disciples have to appear!"[2]

At this point in history, with so much abuse, I'm not sure that that would even do the job. In the Sermon on the Mount, Jesus said, "You are the salt of the earth. But if the salt loses its saltiness, how can it be made salty again? It is no longer good for anything, except to be thrown out and trampled underfoot" (Matthew 5:13). In our world at large, opinion seems to have crystalized. We are being thrown out. We are being trampled underfoot.

In Malachi 2:3, God stated this with even more strength: "Because of you I will rebuke your descendants; I will smear on your faces the dung from your festival sacrifices, and you will be carried off with it." Our failures have left us with dung on our faces, wiped there by God so we get a sense of the stench we have become in the world.

Is there any hope for a church dealing with so much brokenness?

There is hope. Each generation of believers is given an opportunity to tell the story of Jesus through the local church. Regardless of her history, we get to put the brilliance of Jesus on display.

I have written this book to try to stir your faith that God can again use his people to bear witness to his rule and reign. I want to kindle your faith into flame so you will believe that your life can become what Jesus calls it to be. I believe that the time for a rejection of apathy and hopelessness is at hand. The Spirit still hovers over the darkness and chaos in your life, waiting to create something beautiful and compelling. All great revivals have taken place in times of decline. Resurrection is found among the dead. I want to call you to resist compromise when your friends tell you your faith is too intense, your devotion unnecessary, your life together too much. In the following pages, we will contrast things that make for brokenness and things that make for beauty.

I will challenge you to look into your heart and evaluate how you perhaps have been complicit in underplaying the gospel. I'll give you advice, tested in my own life and congregation, for starting to make the journey back to conviction in key areas where we have made compromises. The joy and satisfaction that come from being faithful to Christ will always be richer than the mere ease that comes from drifting along the cultural currents.

I will seek to show you the joys and challenges that come when resistance rises in your heart and formation begins to happen. Together we will examine the depth of the brokenness and seek the antidote. We will examine the contrast in forces and fight for a way forward.

May we take up Bonhoeffer's posture of defiance on the river that day in 1937. May our vision of life together—and faithfulness in following Jesus—be a seed of hope in your life and in the life of our longing world.

THE CONTINUING PROMISE OF THE CHURCH

For the better part of two decades, I have had a complex relationship with the institution called the church. Jesus called her a bride, one of my atheist friends called her a wench, and I have experienced her as both. This duality has caused me to wrestle at a primal level with my faith and my relationship with the church. I am often haunted by the way she doesn't look much like Jesus and why at times I don't either. I have grappled with issues like the exclusive claims of Jesus, historic Christian sexual ethics, the church's complicity in slavery and the oppression of women, violence in the Old Testament, and the church's promiscuity with the systems of the world. I am also grieved by my failures and personal contribution to the staining of her reputation. My own apathy and judgment, my hypocrisy and pride, my failures as a pastor and leader.

But for better or worse, I have been obsessed with the potential of the covenant people of God. I stubbornly believe that the church can be a source of hope and reconciliation in the midst of the world. My love for the church is not a naive love. I have seen the church be a place of breathtaking beauty, and I have seen the church in demonic squalor. The scars on my soul come from the church, as does the joy that has come to define me. Leading in the church has been the source of both the trauma and the consolations in my life.

My perspective on the church is a Western one. I come from a part of the world where I am daily told of the decreasing relevance and accelerating decline of the institution I have given my life to. It's not just the culture walking away from the church; some of my pastor friends have too. They seem to have grown weary of the maintenance of an institution on life support. Why kill themselves to keep this thing going, and for whom? Jesus may still build his church, but they won't be helping.

That's when I remind myself of how history shows that Jesus's commitment to his church is unshakable. Though we have profaned his name among the nations, he retains a passion for his people. We may be hypocrites, we may return to our vomit like dogs, we may embarrass him and distort his message, but the Cross is a covenant Jesus takes seriously. "For better or worse" seems to mean something to the Son of God. Love isn't an idea for God; it's who he is.

The Scriptures give several metaphors for the church that show us Jesus's vision for and commitment to the church. Even in this day, they hold true.

THE CHURCH IS STILL THE BRIDE OF CHRIST

People give their lives away when they fall in love. They surrender their schedules, their finances, even their bodies for the chance to be with the other. Hardened cynics become helpless romantics when they fall in love. Yet many fail to see Jesus's commitment to the church in this light.

Though flawed and broken, the church is the one that Jesus loves. Paul wrote this to the Ephesians: "Husbands, love your wives, just as Christ loved the church and gave himself up for her to make her holy, cleansing her by the washing with water through the word, and to present her to himself as a radiant church, without stain or wrinkle or any other blemish, but holy and blameless" (5:25–27).

Jesus does not view the church simply through a doctrinal, moral, ethical, or sociological lens; he views it through a covenantal lens. Speaker and author Frank Viola noted,

> In Genesis 1 and 2, the Bible opens up with a woman and a man. In Revelation 21 and 22, the Bible closes with a woman and a man. The Bible opens up with a wedding, and it ends with a wedding. It opens with a marriage and it ends with a marriage. . . .
>
> *Your Bible is essentially a love story.*[3]

Jesus is not committed to the church because he has to be; he is committed to the church because he wants to be. God is in love with a woman, and her name is the church.

We see this wedding metaphor from the beginning of redemption. When God used Moses to call the children of Israel into their destiny, he made four promises (Exodus 6:6–7):

- I will take you out.
- I will rescue you.
- I will redeem you.
- I will take you to me.

These four promises were the same four invitations a young man made to a woman on her wedding day. God was not just delivering Israel; he was proposing to her. He called her his "treasured possession" (Exodus 19:5), the same words a groom would use for his bride.[4]

Ezekiel 16 highlights this in even greater detail: "I bathed you with water and washed the blood from you and put ointments on you. I clothed you with an embroidered dress and put sandals of fine leather on you. I dressed you in fine linen and covered you with costly garments. I adorned you with jewelry: I put bracelets on your arms and a necklace around your neck, and I put a ring on your nose, earrings on your ears and a beautiful crown on your head. . . . You became very beautiful and rose to be a queen. And your fame spread among the nations on account of your beauty, because the splendor I had given you made your beauty perfect, declares the Sovereign LORD" (verses 9–14). God has couture taste. His bride will be beautifully adorned.

The challenge of loving a bride like the church is her promiscuous heart. At times she is seduced by the power and grandeur of the world. She often gives her heart to unthinkable ideologies and idolatry, committing adultery with the enemies of Christ. But for whatever reason, God seeks her out, restores her, and brings her back.

This vision of God's passion for the church provides incredible hope. As much as we all have things we hate about the failures of the church, we have been guilty of doing the very things we criticize in her. We have judged and excluded others, we have failed sexually, we have been hypocrites, and we have loved money and power and the praise of people. Yet Jesus still extends his heart and grace to us. Christ seeks us out, welcomes us home, washes away our sin, and showers us with his love.

The church can be beautiful because grace is beautiful. The church can renew her calling because God loves her with undying love. Beauty can resist brokenness because of the passion of the groom. The question is, Will we respond to Jesus's passion for us and be faithful in our generation? Viola continued, "What is the Lord looking for?"

> He is looking for a people who will take their stand in Christ. He's after a people who will dare to believe that they are part of Christ's beloved bride. A people who will defy what they see through their natural eyes and instead look through His eyes. He is looking for a people who see themselves as He sees them, through the prism of divine righteousness, part of a new creation wherein the fall has been eliminated. This is the necessary beginning to fulfilling God's grand mission. To take any other view is to serve God out of guilt, religious duty, or ambition rather than out of love.[5]

THE CHURCH IS STILL THE TEMPLE OF GOD

One of my friends told me that the last place they would ever go to try to find God would be the church. This is nothing short of a tragedy.

The central thing the church is designed to be is a place for his presence. Many of the things we think about when we think about God—law, sacrifice, priests, and theological confessions—were never intended to play the central role they have come to play in our faith today. From the very beginning, God's purpose and passion was to be present with his people. Genesis opens with God in a garden, walking with humanity in the cool of the day (3:8). Most of the things people think of when they think of the church were responses to the fracture of our communion with God and expulsion from his presence. Law, sacrifice, and a priesthood were all ways God's presence had to be mediated because of our sin and brokenness but were not part of God's original design. And all of human history is headed toward restored, intimate, face-to-face relationship with him. In fact, the entire redeemed creation will be a temple of intimate communion. Revelation 21:22–23 says, "I did not see a temple in the city, because the Lord God Almighty and the Lamb are its temple. The city does not need the sun or the moon to shine on it, for the glory of God gives it light, and the Lamb is its lamp."

God's presence among his people has always been his heart. God's vision was not a building to belong in but a people to walk among.[6] Moses, the friend of God, seemed to understand this key point. In a conversation with God while heading to the promised land, he declared that if God's presence did not go with them, they would refuse to leave (Exodus 33:15). Moses asked, "What else will distinguish me and your people from all the other people on the face of the earth?" (verse 16). What else would distinguish them from the nations around them? How about circumcision for a start? How about food restrictions? How about the Sabbath and yearly festivals? How about a list of ethical commandments that would play a defining role in human society for the next 3,500 years? Yet despite these other distinguishing marks, Moses knew that the presence of God was the thing that truly set apart the people of God from the nations around them. The other distinctions were simply social, cultural, and religious boundaries any community could display. But God's presence? That was unmistakable.

At the time of Jesus's ministry, rebuilding of the temple had been underway for forty-six years (John 2:20), and the temple was breathtaking to behold. Its beauty was so well known that the rabbis said, "No one has seen a truly beautiful building unless he has seen the temple."[7] Yet part of the scandal of Jesus's ministry among the Jews was his critique of what the temple had become. After the departure of the glory of God in Ezekiel 10, the temple had been only a symbol, void of substance. It was a religious program without the glorious presence. Jesus called it "a den of robbers" and cleansed it with a whip, turning over the money changers' tables (Matthew 21:12–13; John 2:15). He said it would be torn down and then rebuilt after three days (Matthew 24:1–2; John 2:19–20). His ability to forgive sins on earth rendered the priestly system obsolete. His presence on earth was a threat to a system but salvation for sinners. God's presence had arrived in Christ himself. In fact, this is the great claim of John 1:14: "The Word became flesh and made his dwelling [literally, spread his tent] among us." The presence that departed in Ezekiel was back, but it was in a person, not a place. During the Crucifixion, the veil of the temple was torn in two from top to bottom (Matthew 27:51). God had left the building. It is interesting to note that the temple continued its ministry for about forty more years until the fall of Jerusalem in AD 70. This means that the priests sewed another curtain and put it up to try to keep God in the temple. But it was too late—the Resurrection released the Spirit, and the temple moved from a place to a people.

Through the blood of Jesus Christ and our union with him, *we* have become the temple. Paul said as much to the Corinthian church: "Don't you know that you yourselves are God's temple and that God's Spirit dwells in your midst? If anyone destroys God's temple, God will destroy that person; for God's temple is sacred, and you together are that temple" (1 Corinthians 3:16–17). This is the most incredible claim in human history. The Incarnation meant God with us, but the coming of the Spirit means God in us. Through the death of Jesus on the cross, we have become the place where God dwells. The church is the temple of God, embodying the presence of God on earth.

Can others see that in us?

GOD IN UNEXPECTED PLACES

Our world is often drawn to the visible and prestigious, especially when it comes to the church. Our emphasis on properties and buildings can create a false sense that the building is the temple and that Jesus manifests himself primarily at religiously sanctioned events. But if we are the temple, his presence can be found among us, perhaps especially in the least likely places.

Philip Yancey told a story of one of these encounters while touring a leprosy rehabilitation center in Nepal. Upon entering the Green Pastures Hospital, he noticed one of the ugliest people he had ever seen. Deformed stumps instead of feet, bandaged hands, and a face ravaged by the punishing disease of leprosy. When Yancey looked at the woman's face, instead of a nose, he could see all the way into the sinus cavity. She was completely blind, covered in scars and gauze wrap.

After they were given a tour of the facility, he saw this woman again and realized she had dragged herself along the ground with her elbows like an injured animal. He shared,

> I'm ashamed to say my first thought was, *She's a beggar and she wants money*. My wife, who has worked among the down-and-out, had a much more holy reaction. Without hesitation she bent down to the woman and put her arm around her. The old woman rested her head against Janet's shoulder and began singing a song in Nepali, a tune that we all instantly recognized: "Jesus loves me, this I know, for the Bible tells me so."
>
> "Dahnmaya is one of our most devoted church members," the physical therapist later told us. "Most of our patients are Hindus, but we have a little Christian chapel here, and Dahnmaya comes every time the door opens. She's a prayer warrior. She loves to greet and welcome every visitor who comes to Green Pastures, and no doubt she heard us talking as we walked along the corridor."[8]

In an instant he realized his prejudice had blocked his access to the presence of God in her. This experience reframed his understanding of the church as God's temple in the world. He continued,

> A few months later we heard that Dahnmaya had died. Close to my desk I keep a photo that I snapped just as she was singing to Janet. . . . I see two beautiful women: my wife, smiling sweetly, wearing a brightly colored Nepali outfit she had bought the day before, holding in her

arms an old crone who would flunk any beauty test ever devised except the one that matters most. Out of that deformed, hollow shell of a body, the light of God's presence shines out. The Holy Spirit found a home.[9]

Jesus is committed to his church because he is committed to dwelling among us. And his presence is no longer found on Sinai or Zion but in ordinary people like us.

THE CHURCH IS STILL THE BODY OF CHRIST

I often hear believers say it would be easier to follow Jesus today if he were physically present on earth. I sympathize with this longing. Who hasn't wished Christ would come and settle thousands of years of theological debates and define discipleship for our times? Jesus, however, doesn't seem to have shared this sentiment. In John 16:7, he said that his ascension was for our advantage so that the Helper could come. Jesus wants his followers to grow and have agency, and he prefers partnership to dictatorship in his relationship with us. As C. S. Lewis noted, God "seems to do nothing of Himself which He can possibly delegate to His creatures. He commands us to do slowly and blunderingly what He could do perfectly and in the twinkling of an eye."[10] God wanted not a domain to dominate but a people to partner with. In his vision of tangible presence, Christ has chosen to manifest himself through us.

This was a profound revelation for Paul. When confronting him on the road to Damascus, Jesus asked, "Why do you persecute me?" (Acts 9:4). Yet in Paul's mind he wasn't persecuting Christ, just fanatical followers of a failed rabbi. Yet Jesus implied that to persecute his followers was to persecute him. The head in heaven felt the pains of his body on earth. This revelation transformed Paul's understanding of what the church actually was. In 1 Corinthians 12:27, he wrote, "You are the body of Christ, and each one of you is a part of it." God is looking for a people who want to be filled with his presence and live for his purposes in the world. He wants a surrendered body willing to express his heart and carry out his mission on the earth.

Frank Viola put it this way:

> Evil spirits desire to inhabit human bodies because they crave expression. That's the whole point of possession. They seek to take over a human body so that they can express themselves through it, employing it for wicked purposes on the earth.
>
> Jesus Christ is now in the Spirit. And He craves expression also. He seeks to make His life visible through a many-membered being. . . .
>
> The body of Christ exists to express God in the earth.[11]

OVERCOMING LOCKED-IN SYNDROME

Jean-Dominique Bauby was the French editor of *Elle* magazine and a respected journalist. The father of two, he was known for his sophistication and passion.

One December day his life was disrupted in a jarring way. Only forty-three years old, he suffered a massive stroke that devastated his body. He was in a coma for twenty days, and when he awoke, he found he had lost control of his entire frame. His mouth, arms, and legs would not move. He could not speak or communicate except for one saving grace: he could blink one of his eyes. His mental faculties were completely intact, but he had no way to communicate. Bauby was caught in locked-in syndrome.

In *The Diving Bell and the Butterfly,* the film that tells the story of his life, you see the frustration and determination in Bauby's spirit. One horrific scene shows a doctor sewing one of his eyes shut, while in a voice-over Bauby gives complete and coherent commentary on everything happening to him. When the doctors eventually became aware of what had happened to him, they struggled to find a way to reach the man whose body had become his prison. Bauby ached to communicate, but his whole will, vision, passion, and heart were reduced to the blinking of an eye.

He eventually learned to communicate, but the process was remarkably drawn out. An assistant would recite the alphabet, and when she came to the right letter, Bauby would blink. Then she would recite the alphabet again, and when she reached the right letter, Bauby would blink again. This would happen dozens of times until he spelled out a sentence. Then it would happen hundreds more times until a paragraph was formed. By this excruciatingly slow process, Bauby was able to write his own memoir. *The Diving Bell and the Butterfly* was released to wide acclaim. He tragically died of pneumonia just two days after the book was published.

After watching the film, it's a solemn experience to read the book. You have a sober understanding of the glacial pace of composition, Bauby's frustration with his frail and failing body, and the patience of his assistant faithfully transcribing his work. But the prose is beautiful and moving. Consider his description of his condition: "I am fading away. Slowly but surely. Like the sailor who watches the home shore gradually disappear, I watch my past recede. My old life still burns within me, but more and more of it is reduced to the ashes of memory."[12]

As I finished the film and walked around my neighborhood, I remained in a state of gratitude and wonder at the ease with which my limbs moved. I sat on a bench and consciously moved each muscle slowly, thanking God for my toes, my ankle, my shin, my knee . . . You get the point. As I was sitting there in the warmth of the sun, I was struck by the resemblance between Bauby's situation and God's relationship to his body, the church. In some sense, we suffer from a form of locked-in syndrome. Christ, our head, full of vision, longing, and passion for the world, aches to be able to express himself through a functioning body. But something seems to have happened, some kind of spiritual stroke. Only a portion of our potential is being realized while Jesus blinks out his vision through a fraction of his church.

As I walked home, a prayer rose in my heart, one that has kept me blinking ever since. *Lord, bring your body to life. May it express your heart and passion in a way that reveals the splendor of your salvation to the world.*

Jesus will express himself through us, and slowly but surely, parts of Jesus's body, the church, are coming back to life. In China the church has grown to around 100 million while facing Communist opposition. In Central America the Pentecostal church is living in staggering revival, and in Africa the church has grown at a breathtaking rate in the last hundred years. And hunger is rising in the West. More and more, people I meet are seeking God for revival and are contending like never before. Our resurrecting God is bringing his body to life.

SIGNS OF LIFE

There is a rumor going around the West that, in spite of the avalanche of change and the often-repeated accusation of irrelevance, a church has actually survived. Yes, she is stained; yes, she is broken; but she is here. Her Lord is at work within her. The bride is becoming beautiful; his presence is becoming tangible; the body is becoming functional. Beauty is rising and resisting the brokenness.

He will get the glory. But you and I can be part of the process. I'm not saying it will be easy. Or even safe. If you know how Bonhoeffer came to his end, you know how steep was the cost of his discipleship. But he truly lived while the Lord gave him days on the earth, and his life is still bearing fruit today. Don't you want the same to be said of you?

Doing your part to convert the church from compromise to conviction—to restore her saltiness and turn up her light—is a cause worth giving your life to.

In the chapters ahead, we'll be looking at crucial areas where we must resist compromise in all the beauty of Christlike love and grace. I will address the issues that I feel are most foundational yet also overlooked, ones that will make the biggest difference in your life. I will also try to address them at a deep level. We all know we should love God and love our neighbors (Matthew 22:37–40), but what does that really mean? What does loving God look like with nuance and texture *now*? I believe it looks like worship, rest, and an insatiable spiritual hunger. Likewise, what does it mean to love your neighbor well? I would say it means practicing hospitality, giving honor, loving our enemies, making sacrifices, and celebrating God's goodness together.

A church pursuing that could *actually* start a beautiful resistance.

Chapter 2

Worship Must Resist Idolatry

We resemble what we revere, either for ruin or restoration.

G. K. BEALE, *We Become What We Worship*

Those who worship worthless idols forfeit the mercy that could be theirs.

Jonah 2:8, NET

I grew up in a home with godly parents. Quiet, conservative people, they were committed to prayer and sincere in their faith. From the outside, they were not emotionally excessive, and they had small hobbies they enjoyed. My dad made and collected model cars, while my mother loved to spend time in the garden. But despite their apparent ordinariness, there was something about my parents' faith that few people knew. In their spare time, my parents cast out demons. These quiet, faithful people—unsuspected by most—moved in tremendous spiritual power and led people in deliverance.

This resulted in some interesting encounters in my house as I was growing up. One day I noticed that my father seemed exhausted when he got home. I asked him where he had been and why he looked so tired.

His reply—something I did not see coming—has stuck with me over the years. "Well," he said, "we've been working with a woman who has a demon inside her. We have fasted and prayed, but we just can't seem to get a break-through. The demon won't leave."

"Oh," I replied and walked out of the room. I had no idea what to make of a day like that. Demons? Breakthrough? Fasting?

The next day my father came home and his countenance was light. I asked, "How did it go today?"

He replied, "We found the source of the stronghold and were able to de-stroy it. This woman had a relationship with a man, a former lover. Turns out, she kept a record with their song on it. The man had become her god, an idol. That record was the point of access in idolizing the relationship. That song be-came a stronghold. When she destroyed the record, its hold was broken."

I have often reflected on this encounter in my pastoral ministry. Many times while living in New York, I have seen people worship their careers and accomplishments with a kind of religious devotion that would put the strict-est fundamentalist to shame. Or they worship wealth and its accumulation. Or love and sex. Or freedom. Or image. It's more or less the same all over. And no one seems to blink an eye.

We live in a society without a reference point for idolatry. We have neither the cultural framework nor the worldview to support it. And this makes us all the more susceptible to it. Bruce Ellis Benson, a former professor of philosophy, wrote, "Not only are we capable of creating idols and worshiping them, we are likewise capable of being almost or completely blind to their existence. . . . Our recognition of idols for what they are is often selective."[1]

It's amazing how clearly we can see false worship in others. Yet in our own lives, idolatry comes to feel normal, like an enjoyable hobby, a rational ap-proach, the way things simply are. Yet these idols have the power to enslave us.

Hard work is good. The same can be said of love, family, fitness, sports, church, and so many other things we idolize. In their place and in proportion, they are all good—but not one of them is God.

Idolatry is worship of an unworthy object. The countercultural, revolu-tionary act is to direct our hearts' deepest devotion toward—and *only* toward—

the Creator of our beings. "True worshipers will worship the Father in the Spirit and in truth" (John 4:23). Right worship has the power to put our lives back on course and, in the process, expose the misplaced priorities of a culture gone rotten.

Worship must resist idolatry.

THE REALITY OF IDOLATRY TODAY

We're discussing an old, old topic here. Idolatry has been a pernicious reality for the people of God in every age. Consider the way the Enemy first tempted humanity: "You will be like God" (Genesis 3:5). It was an invitation to make an idol out of self and make ourselves equal with God. This same temptation is whispered in the ears of us all.

Consider next the golden calf (Exodus 32:1–6). The idolatry at the foot of Sinai seems unthinkable. We are often prone to believe that if we saw more of God's power—a legitimate miracle—we would never doubt again. Yet the Israelites had seen incredible miracles: judgment on the Egyptian gods, reparations for their four hundred years of slavery, and the parting of the Red Sea. Then, while Moses was seeking God on their behalf and receiving the Ten Commandments, they took the wealth of Egypt, given by God to lay the foundation of their new economy, and had Aaron turn it into a pagan statue. Aaron then cried out to the people, "These are your gods, Israel, who brought you up out of Egypt" (verse 4).

Sadly, that sort of thing happened again and again in the Bible. This should produce deep caution and humility in us. Instead of thinking, *That was then; this is now,* we need to be aware of our hearts' tendency toward the same thing. Theologian William Stringfellow commented, "Idolatry is pervasive in every time and culture, no less now than yesterday, no less in Washington than Gomorrah. . . . Indeed, it might be argued that contemporary Western man is more enslaved to idols than his supposedly less civilized counterpart precisely because he is, presumably, less ignorant about the world in which he lives, and because his favorite idols are the familiar realities of daily life—religion, work, money, status, sex, patriotism."[2]

Disordered Loves

With such strong warnings about idolatry as we find in Scripture, it's important to clarify what we mean. In Romans 1:21, Paul provided the root of idolatry: "Although they knew God, they neither glorified him as God nor gave thanks to him." Their lives and loves had gotten out of order. Created things got in the way of the Creator. Gratitude turned into entitlement.

The Scriptures are all about getting the right things in the right order. "You shall have no other gods before me" (Exodus 20:3). "Love the Lord your God with all your heart and with all your soul and with all your mind and with all your strength" (Mark 12:30; see Deuteronomy 6:5). Jesus also commanded his disciples not to run after the things pagans run after (Matthew 6:32). They were to "seek first the kingdom of God" (verse 33, ESV). Worship is about the priorities of our hearts.

Idols, then, are the wicked fruit of disordered loves. The Westminster Larger Catechism states that the first commandment is violated when there is an "inordinate and immoderate setting of our mind, will, or affections upon other things."[3] It is putting something before God. Tim Keller, for years my fellow Manhattan pastor, put it like this: "We think that idols are bad things, but that is almost never the case. The greater the good, the more likely we are to expect that it can satisfy our deepest needs and hopes. Anything can serve as a counterfeit god, especially the very best things in life. . . . [An idol] is anything more important to you than God."[4]

The persistent temptation is to turn *good things* into *God things*. Even people who don't claim a religion worship something as if they did. There's something absorbing their hearts and passion, driving and filling their lives. As biblical counselor Elyse Fitzpatrick asked, "How can I tell if I'm worshiping the blessings that I desire or God? . . . If you're willing to sin to obtain your goal or if you sin when you don't get what you want, then your desire has taken God's place and you're functioning as an idolater."[5] Is there anything in your life you want badly enough that you're willing to violate Scripture or your own conscience? Are you using sin to medicate the absence of something you truly want?

In our modern world, with its temptations, our desires get so easily entangled. This inner confusion brings disaster into our lives. We begin to expect created things to meet our needs as they were never designed to do.

One Christian philosopher got to the root of this reality well:

God is one thing, angels are another, as are people, terriers, red oaks, squash, rocks, and dirt. Each item fits in God's overall scheme of creation. The nature of things in the hierarchy is unchangeable, and so is the kind of satisfaction it can provide when we are related to it through love.

Because of these actual differences in things, the outcome of loving each actual thing will be different. There is a divinely designed fit between our needs, the character of the things that can satisfy them, and the way we should love them in order to be satisfied. Even though each thing God made is good, delightful, legitimate, and a source of satisfaction as an object of our love, we "must not expect more from it than its unique nature can provide." We must give love and praise to things apportioned to their worth.

Problems don't arise because we need things, or because we love things. . . . Problems arise when we fail to grasp the *nature* of the objects that we need and love . . . and the *expectations* we have regarding the outcome of our love.[6]

Disordered loves lead to disordered lives. "They neither glorified him as God nor gave thanks to him" (Romans 1:21). Instead, they worshipped created things. This is the root of idolatry.

TEMPTATIONS FILLING US AND SURROUNDING US

So that you may start peering around your blind spots and identifying your own idols, let me help you consider the categories. In 1 John 2:15–17, John talked about two kinds of idols: "Do not love the world or anything in the world. If anyone loves the world, love for the Father is not in them. For everything in the world—the lust of the flesh, the lust of the eyes, and the pride of life—comes not from the Father but from the world. The world and its desires pass away, but whoever does the will of God lives forever." Here we see . . .

- *Heart idols*—things that we elevate to pseudodivinity in our hearts
- *Cultural idols*—things the world values that seize our affection and devotion

Heart Idols

In a fascinating passage in Ezekiel 14, some of the elders of Israel went up to the prophet Ezekiel to hear a message from the Lord. That sounds like a godly, faithful thing to do, right? But what did the Lord say about this? "These men have set up idols in their hearts and put wicked stumbling blocks before their faces. Should I let them inquire of me at all?" (verse 3). In other words, "Forget it! As long as these people have idols in their hearts, I'm not going to lead them. Instead of prophecy, here is what I have to say to them: 'Repent! Turn from your idols.'"

As we approach God, his primary concern is the devotion of our hearts, not our performance out of duty. It's incredibly easy to have something take over our hearts, to make its way into first place without our even knowing it. We can keep up involvement in our small groups, attend church faithfully, give generously, and love sacrificially, while holding something other than God as sacred in our hearts. That's why God always looks first at our hearts rather than our religious habits.

You can see this in the Ten Commandments. These are often misunderstood as an external law designed to modify our behavior. But actually, the commandments start with our hearts and direct us to love before they move outward to morality. David Powlison, in a much-quoted essay on idolatry, said, "The First Great Commandment, to 'love God heart, soul, mind, and might,' also demonstrates the essential 'inward-ness' of the law regarding idolatry."[7]

When something takes the place of God, our loves get distorted. Sometimes that thing is money and financial success. Maybe it's our intelligence, sexuality, power, or even the fear of people. There's almost an endless list of things that can function as a god, a *heart idol*. Heart idols are those things we put before God in our values, affections, and minds. Is there anything you have set in your heart this way?

I was speaking with a young man in our church whose life was controlled by a heart idol. On the outside his life looked almost perfect. Private schools while growing up, an Ivy League college education, a noted graduate school degree. He served and gave and led in our church and was widely respected by all. Yet those who knew him below the surface realized something wasn't quite right. He was incredibly defensive and unable to take criticism. He would either turtle up or lash out. He was defensive in a disproportionate way when challenged.

I spent some time walking with him and developed a real level of trust. One day he confided that his whole life was one giant quest for approval. He wanted the blessing of a father who had never given it to him. He wanted to be so successful and accomplished that his dad was forced to bless him. Anytime he felt challenged, he worried that it would set him back, and his fear was revealed. His heart idol of approval hid behind a successful exterior.

Cultural Idols

In the Greco-Roman world, every region had local deities. These gods were at the center of the culture, defining things like fashion, identities, and societal rhythms. Perhaps the idea of regional gods sounds primitive, yet in our own

day every place has a culture—a mix of values, traditions, rituals, and expectations that makes it unique. Sometimes cultural idols are obvious, casting a
shadow over the region; sometimes they are more subtle. Consider New York,
where I live. Our sports teams often mimic regional deities. We love our local
teams and despise our enemies. You would see this clearly if you wore a
Boston Red Sox shirt and wandered into the Yankees stadium during a game.
That could have real-world consequences. Though seemingly small, these
can be cultural tells of deeper realities. They are what anthropologist Mary
Douglas called "condensed symbols," small things that have larger embodied
meaning.[8]

Good cultural things like career or financial security, when elevated to first
place, can create a complex system hard to detect and resist. Sociologist Peter
Berger developed the idea of "plausibility structures," how we perceive the
world, real and valuable, based on where we live.[9] We instinctively look to a
peer reference group to disciple us and instruct us in how to be acceptable in
each setting. These groups become our relational and behavioral dashboards,
letting us know where we fit in and what we need to change to receive approval
and acceptance.

We humans have little cultural antennae always shooting off signals to
gauge whether we belong. *How do I fit in? How do I live? What's valued here?*
We read, adjust, and conform. These external forces can exert tremendous pressure on how we act.

In the same way that a Christian is discipled by the believing community
into the image of Jesus, our world seeks to disciple and form us into its image.
We may be blind to many of these cultural idols, but if we look at our culture
with eyes enlightened by the Spirit and the Word, we can begin to see the
reality.

This often manifests itself in New York around the idol of money. New
York is a place where people can make $2 million on Wall Street and still feel
they have hardly enough money to get by. Between the private school pay-
ments, the nanny, the house at the beach, and the apartment mortgage, a per-

son may ache for more, blind to the fact that he or she is within the top 0.05 percent of all earners in recorded history.

Mammon makes us look up at those above us in envy, not down to those below us with gratitude for what we have. This cultural idol distorts our view of reality.

Conservatives have traditionally focused on heart idols, while liberals have focused on cultural idols. We then pit our forms of idolatry against each other and moralize the gods we have chosen to serve. But Jesus wants his followers to care about justice *and* holiness, orphans and widows, *and* being unpolluted by the world (James 1:27). We need a kingdom vision that transcends these categories of idolatry and offers an alternative vision. It is only when worshipping believers resist all idolatry that they can truly be an alternative community of hope, anointed by God to bring renewal to the world at large.

NEW YORK CREDIBILITY

When I moved to New York to plant a church, I was pretty sure my motives were right. I wanted to see God's kingdom come in power. I wanted to see those far from God find redemption and freedom in him. But New York holds a cultural power that shapes the heart more than I ever anticipated.

People have been coming to this city for decades with a single vision: to seek recognition and reward. To facilitate this, an entire ecosystem of power and approval has been established to administer cultural success. Institutions and corporations and taste makers and cultural shapers dictate the terms of success and the rewards of recognition. This external influence can exert tremendous power on even the sincerest heart. People who live here know the way the city can cast a spell over a soul. One of the chief ways this happens is through the idea of being seen as credible in the city.

After giving it all we had—prayer, time, money, and relationship—our church was doing well. Well enough to attract the attention of one of the city's major newspapers. One Easter it did a feature article on our church and its vision for the city. Though not horrific, it treated us as sophomoric outsiders, naive well-wishers who hadn't really come to terms with what we were doing or what the city wanted. That report on our church spread through several other media outlets, garnering local attention and putting us on the map. But the feedback was harsh.

This caused an interior crisis the like of which I had never experienced before—a crisis of approval. How would we reach people if we were not taken seriously? What were we doing wrong that made the city dismiss us so easily? Was it possible to present the gospel in a sophisticated and not sophomoric way and be seen as more credible, all without compromising the gospel?

Over the next few months, the idol of approval formed in my heart. A new lens filtered everything I saw and did—the lens of cultural acceptance. Is this offensive to New Yorkers? Is our worship too emotional, our preaching too sentimental, our language too triumphalist, our theology too conservative? And slowly the desire for contextualization began to bleed with small drops of compromise. Instead of focusing on what Jesus thought of the church, I became city focused.

This was the common thread of compromise in most of the churches in Revelation 2–3. They let the culture shape their calling, and Jesus rebuked them. Some of Jesus's harshest words in all Scripture are reserved for the church that cares more about the opinion of the world than his own.

One Sunday, during a worship service, I sat at the back of the room. I was angry and frustrated. The service felt too kitschy, too southern, too out of place in a neighborhood like this. I wanted to yell at the team that no one would take us seriously if we did church like this. The idol of approval was strangling the Spirit in my life.

And suddenly I realized what had been happening inside me.

I began to weep there on the back pew. I was overwhelmed and frustrated at how something so small as an article in a paper could exert such pressure on my heart. In that moment I felt Jesus convict me deeply. "This is not your church. It's mine. If you only allow what is acceptable in the eyes of the city, you will quench the work I want to do. You will have a church the city thinks is respectable but I find wanting. You will have a church more informed by New York cultural preferences than my Word."

It was a devastating critique, but the strength of the impression and the truth it contained opened my eyes to my disordered loves. A heart idol was giving in to cultural idols, and the combination was robbing our church of its power.

I came to a place of deep repentance that night and took a hammer to that idol in my heart. I saw how tragic it was to seek the blessing of the world at the expense of the anointing of God. And that repentance created space for a fresh work of the Spirit. It's not that I don't struggle with a desire for acceptance anymore (every heart does), but the functional power of that idol is gone, drowned out by a louder voice and responsibility in my heart. To seek his kingdom first and love him rightly—that's the deepest cry of my heart.

THE DEADLINESS OF IDOLS

I shudder to think what would have happened if I had continued on the road of bowing down to approval instead of to Christ. Although Bonhoeffer and the Finkenwalders found a community of faithfulness, many of their fellow German Christians hid the light of truth while the Nazis reigned.

Why are idols so deadly? Because they deceive, distort, and destroy. Heart idols distort our lives. Cultural idols distort our world.

Deception
Paul stated in Romans 1:21, "Their thinking became futile." The problem with deception is that you don't know you are being deceived. It simply feels as if you're right. Deception feels incredibly rational. Idols function like spiritual forgeries, imitating God's character but distorting it. That's why theology is not

merely for people in seminary. It's important for all God's people to know who God is so we can spot counterfeit gods when they approach our lives.

Idols give promises and warnings, and both the promises and the warnings are lies. Giving in to these promises will disillusion you, and heeding the warnings will harm you. False gods create false law, false definitions of success and failure, false definitions of value and stigma. Idols define good and evil contrary to God's definitions. They deceive us.

Distortion

Second, idols distort us. We don't just think differently; we become different people. Romans 1:21 again: "Their foolish hearts were darkened." Something happens on the inside that works its way out in our lives. This is why Psalm 115:8 states, "Those who make [idols] will be like them, and so will all who trust in them."

Isn't it amazing how, when people discover a new passion, it begins to affect everything they do? People change their clothing, adjust their schedules, fill their vocabulary with new words. They adjust their budgets, friendships, and other relationships to align with the thing that has captured their hearts. Participation brings formation. Over time we are shaped by the things we serve. If we begin to serve idols, terrible distortion can happen.

Novelist David Foster Wallace said, "Pretty much anything . . . you worship will eat you alive." He went on to say that if you worship money and things, you will never have enough. If you worship beauty and sexual allure, you will feel ugly. If you worship power, you will feel weak and afraid. If you worship intelligence, you will end up feeling stupid.[10]

Destruction

Ultimately, this progression results in our destruction. Look at Romans 1:18: "The wrath of God is being revealed from heaven against all the godlessness and wickedness of people, who suppress the truth by their wickedness." Many in the church today try hard to edit out the wrath of God. It's important to understand, however, that this is an essential response of God to the evil and injustice in our world.

Wrath actually has a wide semantic range. The wrath spoken of here is not like our mercurial wrath. Paul said, "God gave them over" (verse 24). This is not God striking out in anger. It's God's passive wrath, saying something like "You don't want me to be God? Fine. Do your own thing. Be your own gods and see how that goes."

Living under the judgment of our own idolatry will demonstrate that truth and righteousness really do bring healing and restoration.

In America, we're feeling the consequences of worshipping idols rather than God. Take, for example, the idol of mammon. Serving mammon led to a financial collapse in 2008 that brought widespread destruction and despair. In an article in the *New Yorker,* George Packer talked about this destruction: "When the crash came . . . , it wiped out nine million jobs, took away nine million homes, erased retirement accounts. . . . The Great Recession that accompanied the financial crisis didn't bring back breadlines or industrial strikes. This time, the desperation was quiet and lonely: a pile of mail at the doorstep of a deserted house; . . . a middle-aged man playing video games all day; . . . a retired woman trying to get a human being on the phone at the bank."[11] The sadness, loneliness, and isolation were how the god of mammon repaid those who had served it. The greed of many caused heartache for us all, as some of the most vulnerable in society were crushed by the economic collapse.

This is why God urges us not to serve the things that we create. In Isaiah 44:15–17, God lamented how the craftsman makes a fire with half his wood and then builds an idol out of the other half. Oh, the futility! That's why the language in Jeremiah 2 is so intense:

> "Has a nation ever changed its gods?
>   (Yet they are not gods at all.)
> But my people have exchanged their glorious God
>   for worthless idols.

Be appalled at this, you heavens,
  and shudder with great horror,"
    declares the LORD.
"My people have committed two sins:
They have forsaken me,
  the spring of living water,
and have dug their own cisterns,
  broken cisterns that cannot hold water." (verses 11–13)

We suppress the truth in unrighteousness, and as a result, our idols eat us alive. God's heart is that we know him and live in freedom and joy. This is why he calls us to tear down these spiritual forgeries so that we can enjoy the goodness of his love. The antidote for idolatry is rightly ordering our loves. It's getting our hearts, our minds, our souls, and our strength oriented toward the thing that can truly satisfy.

RESPONDING TO IDOLATRY THE WRONG WAY

The apostle John closed one of his epistles with the short statement "Dear children, keep yourselves from idols" (1 John 5:21). What an interesting way to close an epistle! Of all the things on the apostle's heart at that moment, this was his great appeal. As followers of Jesus were navigating the empire, he called them to a faithful resistance.

So, how do we keep ourselves from idols in our modern secular age? How do we resist?

People have instinctively realized the destructive power of idols, and they search and grasp for a way out from their tyranny. This is normally manifested in two ineffective responses.

The first is the *religious response,* focusing on human wisdom and self-righteousness.

Religion relies on self-effort to try to overcome idols. It is futile. All religion does is reinforce idolatry. It's an attempt to fight secular idols with religious ones. Rather than changing the heart, it seeks to bludgeon it into submission.

Parents often unintentionally do this with their children. They use one idol against another to try to control their kids. They discipline their children with shame ("How could you be so rude?") or bait them with pride ("Don't you want everyone to think you are a wonderful little girl?") rather than addressing the deep issue, teaching them loving respect for and humble submission to authority.

This was the approach of the Pharisees, who used religious pride and shame to maintain control and manipulate the behavior of others. This turned a covenant of life into a culture of death. Jesus described them as whitewashed tombs that look good on the outside but are full of dead people's bones (Matthew 23:27).

The second response is the *secular response*. It trades a dysfunctional idol for a more functional idol.

I read an account of a woman who was seeing a secular therapist. She was in a bad relationship and couldn't understand why she couldn't break free. During this process, she encountered Jesus and began to grow as a Christian. She began to hear her therapist through the lens of the gospel and realized the futility of the framework being offered to her.

"He's not worthy of you. Say to yourself, 'I'm worthy of better,'" she was told. "You've got low self-esteem because of how this man is treating you. You need to finish that master's degree you've always wanted. You need to be an independent woman that doesn't need men."

But she came to realize that her idol was her need for a man to make her feel good about herself and that independence was simply another form of idolatry. The therapist wanted her to trade a dysfunctional idol for a more functional idol. So the woman said, "I think I'm treating the symptoms and not the root." She was able to let God's grace into the deep places of pain and brokenness and learned to be content in the Father's love. She didn't need a more functional idol; she needed a revelation of the One who died to set her free.

Christians do not replace one idol with another. We repent from all idolatry. We replace our idols with the wonder of the true and unconditional love that is ours in Christ.

RESPONDING TO IDOLATRY THE RIGHT WAY

In the US legal system, there is a concept that legal philosopher H. L. A. Hart called "the ultimate rule of recognition." Any legislation passed in the United States must line up with the Constitution. For Americans, the Constitution is the ultimate rule of recognition.

All of us need a rule of recognition in our own hearts. We need to make sure that all our loves and longing are centered on God. This means loyalty in every area of life: money, sexuality, careers, and time. He is our ultimate rule of recognition.

That's why church matters. Western culture is a seductive environment, with many cultural idols working on our affections and practices, changing our habits and shaping our minds. The church exists as a counterformative community to confront our idolatry. So we don't go to church for entertainment. No, what we're really working for here is transformation into the image of Jesus. This is why Philip Yancey stated, "Church exists primarily not to provide entertainment . . . or to build self-esteem or to facilitate friendships but to worship God; if it fails in that, it fails. I have learned that . . . the ultimate goal [is] getting worshipers in touch with God."[12]

There are two areas of application: our hearts (we tear down personal idols) and the church (we resist cultural idols).

Giving God Our Hearts

The apostle Paul stated, "I am jealous for you with a godly jealousy. I promised you to one husband, to Christ, so that I might present you as a pure virgin to him. But I am afraid . . . your minds may somehow be led astray from your sincere and pure devotion to Christ" (2 Corinthians 11:2–3). Paul was passionate to see God's people love the right things, the right way. This was his whole goal.

Before I met my wife and married her, I loved other women. My wife loved other men before she met me. At our wedding, we said the following words as a declaration over our whole lives, past, present, future: "forsaking all others." Imagine what would happen if I kept a box of mementos of all the women I loved before I met my wife. Then whenever I felt sad or wanted to celebrate or deal with my struggles, I pulled them out and dredged up memories of my previous relationships. My marriage would not go well.

This is essentially what idolatry of the heart is. Jesus is Lord . . . except over my sexuality or money. Jesus is Lord . . . except in moments of stress when I resort to control or manipulation.

We must forsake all others out of loyalty to him.

God is not interested in our behavior. Moralism says behavior is foremost. Secularism thinks character traits are foremost. But God wants our hearts. Until we see idolatry as spiritual adultery, we will be prone to dismiss it. If you get your heart right, everything will follow. We need to make sure that in our times of stress and sorrow and in the celebration of our triumphs, we turn our hearts to God in gratitude and prayer and worship, inviting him into the places of anxiety and fear, rather than medicating them by looking to some temporary solution. Netflix and pizza feel like a wonderful comfort at the moment, but if we use these to fend off dependence on God, we delay our deliverance.

God is at war for the love of your heart.

Disrupting Cultural Idolatry Through Devotion

In order for the church to function as an alternative community of freedom and hope, we have to discern the forces that conspire to establish idols in our hearts. Then we must resist and replace them. That's why worship is such an important part of our common life. We need weekly opportunities of confession, formation, and Scripture to rightly order our hearts and loves and release fresh wonder in our relationship with God. Worship is a kind of liminal space in our world that creates room for reflection and repentance.

King David prayed in Psalm 139:23–24,

> Search me, God, and know my heart;
> > test me and know my anxious thoughts.
> See if there is any offensive way in me,
> > and lead me in the way everlasting.

This submission of our hearts to the Lord and the searching of the Spirit can function as a sort of spiritual MRI, revealing the motives of our hearts below the surface of our behavior. We can then repent of the idols that have influenced us and invite the Spirit to cleanse us. When this happens, the gospel is seen as good news because it saves us from having to save ourselves or serve another master and reminds us of our call to live in the freedom of the love and approval of God.

That's why we cannot let busy travel schedules, kids' sporting events, vacations, holidays, and personal preferences take priority over our call to worship. If we are not careful, without meaning to, we will "giv[e] up meeting together, as some are in the habit of doing" (Hebrews 10:25). This means we become more shaped by the rhythms of the culture than the gospel, and our hearts are prone to wander.

James K. A. Smith, Canadian American philosopher, noted, "Christian worship is one of the primary arenas in which we participate in the practices that shape who we are. If our worship simply mimics the disciplinary practices and goals of a consumer culture, we will not be formed otherwise. Conceiving of the church as a disciplinary society aimed at forming human beings to reflect the image of Christ, we will offer an alternative society to the hollow formations of late-modern culture."[13] To paraphrase missiologist Lesslie Newbigin, we must live in the kingdom of God in such a way that it provokes questions for which the gospel is the answer.[14] When we seek first the kingdom of God, love him with our whole hearts, and prize our loyalty to him, a watching world will be compelled to ask about the difference they see in our lives.

The Power of Worship

Whenever the church gathers and offers its collective heart in worship, powerful things can happen. The Father is seen for who he is, and the soul is stirred. Christ is seen in ascended glory, and the heart rejoices. The Spirit is poured out, resulting in our transformation and empowerment to seek God more.

For Bonhoeffer, this was why worship was so central at Finkenwalde. "Though we live in the world, we do not wage war as the world does. The weapons we fight with are not the weapons of the world. On the contrary, they have divine power to demolish strongholds. We demolish arguments and every pretension that sets itself up against the knowledge of God, and we take captive every thought to make it obedient to Christ" (2 Corinthians 10:3–5). Even though a small group of pastors on the outskirts of Germany seemed like nothing compared with the power of the Reich, the power of the gospel overcame the power of the Reich.

And this is why our worship matters, wherever we are.

When you gather in Jesus's name, no matter how large or small the assembly, you are bearing witness before the powers that be that you cannot be bought. Your heart will remain steadfast, your resistance potent, and your vision glorious. Repentance and worship become your rhythm, and idols are resisted and replaced. Tiny outposts of worship can defy principalities, reconcile communities, transform history. God is at war for the love of your heart. May your worship resist idolatry.

Chapter 3

Rest Must Resist Exhaustion

I didn't know I was allowed to rest.

LYNNE M. BAAB, *Sabbath Keeping*

This is what the Sovereign LORD, the Holy One of Israel, says:
"In repentance and rest is your salvation,
in quietness and trust is your strength."

Isaiah 30:15

ack in the 1980s, Kamei Shuji was a Japanese business prodigy. After graduating from college, he started working for the Osaka branch of Ace Securities, a respected brokerage firm. Like most recent graduates, he was assigned to external sales, the hardest and least rewarding branch of the company. Kamei was given the task of cold-calling potential clients. The scheduled hours were 8:40 a.m. to 5:00 p.m., Monday through Friday. But he found that he simply could not generate enough leads in the time allotted. So he began to work harder. He changed his schedule to 6:50 a.m. to 10:00 p.m., seven days a week.

Blessed with mental fortitude and physical stamina, he became a rising star in his generation of Japanese stockbrokers. Success was his vision, performance his life. And he made it. He earned inclusion in the legendary *kigyō senshi* (corporate warriors), and he was honored in corporate publications.

Younger traders idolized Shuji and aspired to be like him. He regularly worked ninety-hour weeks, averaging thirteen hours a day, seven days a week. When the Nikkei bubble began to burst, he put in even more hours to try to cover his losses. Shuji was all in. Shuji was crushing it.

Shuji is dead.

During a weekend sales seminar at a resort, he collapsed and died from a myocardial infarction. His heart simply gave out. He was twenty-six years old.[1]

Kamei Shuji was not the first to die on the job. In Japan this has happened with such frequency that it has been diagnosed as a medical condition. *Karōshi.* Death by overwork.

Decades later, it appears we have not learned a thing. In some sense, Kamei Shuji's work approach has become normal life in American culture. "No large country in the world as productive as the United States averages more hours of work a year. And the gap between the U.S. and other countries is growing. Between 1950 and 2012, annual hours worked per employee fell by about 40 percent in Germany and the Netherlands—but by only 10 percent in the United States."[2] Similarly, political scientist Samuel P. Huntington said that Americans "work longer hours, have shorter vacations, get less in unemployment, disability, and retirement benefits, and retire later, than people in comparably rich societies."[3]

Not only is work dominating our schedules, but it is also affecting our health. Physicians have noted the connection between stress and health: "Generally, stressful events are thought to influence the patho-genesis of physical disease by causing . . . feelings of anxiety and depression, which in turn exert direct effects on biological processes or behavioral patterns that influence disease risk. Exposures to chronic stress are considered the most toxic because they are the most likely to result in long-term or permanent changes in the emotional, physiological, and behavioral responses that influence susceptibility to and course of disease."[4]

Our busyness is destroying our peace, eliminating margin, and deeply affecting our bodies. Whether C-suite executives or stay-at-home moms, we all feel perpetually overwhelmed. We are experiencing karōshi in slow motion. Our pace of life and obsession with accomplishing more are also touching our souls. Many today are suffering from a form of spiritual karōshi. Our souls are slowly dying from being overwhelmed and neglected.

The Maker of our bodies knows their limitations and what overwork can do to us. And that is one reason that, from the beginning, he impressed a rhythm of alternating work and rest into time. His regular rest is the Sabbath, and we consider it outdated at our peril. In a world of nonstop pursuit of achievement, men and women who are willing to let go of their tools and rest—not merely for self-care but to retune their hearts to God's calling—are going to stand out. They're going to be prophetic witnesses that having it all is really having nothing if we don't have a life.

For followers of Jesus, rest is both our present reality and our destiny (Hebrews 4:1–11). Rest must resist exhaustion.

BURNED OUT AND BURDENED

People of faith have long noted Jesus's invitation to let him ease the burdens of life. I wrote a whole book—*The Burden Is Light*—calling people back to this beautiful vision. Echoing through history, Jesus's invitation seems timelier and more compelling than ever. "Come to me, all you who are weary and burdened, and I will give you rest" (Matthew 11:28). For many, life has come to be defined by these categories—labor and burden, busyness and burnout. Our modern work ethic, schedules, and ambition have become a burden, under the weight of which we all seem to stagger. There doesn't seem to be a category of life in which exhaustion doesn't define us.

In Praise of Slowness author Carl Honoré recounted an incident that woke him up to the absurdities of the pace and aggression of modern life. While waiting in line in an airport, he read a newspaper article about a book entitled

One-Minute Bedtime Stories. In this book, the authors had condensed classic children's stories into sixty-second sound bites. Honoré said, "Think Hans Christian Andersen meets the executive summary."[5]

Honoré noted his internal tension. A part of him thought, *At last! A faster, simpler way to get kids down at night.* At the same time, he was horrified to realize that he was trying to optimize his time to avoid the frustrations of bed-time rituals. Rather than pursuing deep intimacy and connection with his son, he was tempted to grab at a shortened version of parenting so he could have a shortened version of his son's childhood.

To be honest, we have all felt this kind of tension. We all long to shift be-yond the craziness of our lives yet realize we are rarely willing to touch the rhythms and habits that create the need for simplification in the first place. In the end, rather than time being a gift, it becomes a tyrant, and tyrants control through violence. Trappist monk Thomas Merton wrote, "To allow oneself to be carried away by a multitude of conflicting concerns, to surrender to too many demands, to commit oneself to too many projects, to want to help every-one in everything is to succumb to violence."[6] We may ache for peace in the world, but many of our lifestyles are a form of violence to ourselves and those we love.

As a pastor in one of America's most work-obsessed cities, I have begun to detect a subtle and seductive lie making its way into our modern thinking, one that has wrought destruction on us all. It's what I call the *stressful season with-out consequences.* Many people move to the city with a vision of success, in terms of both recognition and financial reward, but to really achieve this, peo-ple have to put forth extraordinary effort. The hours required, the energy ex-pended, and the demands placed on the body and heart can be so intense that the inner life begins to wither. "It will just be for a year or two," the narrative says, but the kind of cultural formation and spiritual deformation that can take place in that amount of time is staggering. Values are distorted, vision blurred, idols established, identity shifted, and relationships strained. This way of living shifts out of a season because ambition demands it, and the lie becomes a lifestyle.

When lies become lifestyles, your days are numbered. A. J. Swoboda wrote,

> Our time-saving devices, technological conveniences, and cheap mobility have seemingly made life much easier and interconnected. As a result, we have more information at our fingertips than anyone in history. Yet with all this progress, we are ominously dissatisfied. In bowing at these sacred altars of hyperactivity, progress, and technological compulsivity, our souls increasingly pant for meaning and value and truth as they wither away, exhausted, frazzled, displeased, ever on edge. . . . Our bodies wear ragged. Our spirits thirst. We have an inability to simply sit still and *be*. As we drown ourselves in a 24/7 living, we seem to be able to do anything *but* quench our true thirst for the life of God. . . .
>
> The result . . . is that we have become perhaps the most emotionally exhausted, psychologically overworked, spiritually malnourished people in history.[7]

Could it be possible to recover the nourishment we're missing?

THIRD SOIL CULTURE

I believe that, deep in our hearts, we genuinely desire to please God. We do long for lives of intimacy and fruitfulness, but our cultural setting demands the highest levels of vigilance if this is going to happen. We will not drift into devotion or glide into godliness.

Jesus warns us about the challenges we will face if we want this kind of life. In the parable of the sower, he described four kinds of soil. I am sure you are familiar with the gist of the parable, but are you as familiar with the forms the soil can take in your life? Describing the third kind of soil, Jesus spoke about how "the worries of this life and the deceitfulness of wealth choke the word, making it unfruitful" (Matthew 13:22). The things that overwhelm us and rob us of intimacy and fruitfulness don't manifest themselves as grave spiritual threats aiming to rob us of our destiny. They just seem like, well, life. Travel sports on weekends that rob us of local and religious connection, season 3 of _____ on Netflix that takes time away from listening to our neighbors, relentlessly checking social media, which cultivates envy and erodes compassion. These things subtly seduce us and distort our vision of life. They take up the space required for the gospel to thrive.

In this parable Jesus was using a farming metaphor. There is no Monsanto for the spiritual life. Like the seed, the gospel takes time to bear fruit. It takes intentional cultivation. The cares and deception don't storm in; they sneak in. But once present, they strangle us and shift us from an eternal to an immediate focus, distorting and disordering our priorities. It's hard to think about eternity and the kingdom of God when you are gasping for air. It's hard to think about anything but your next breath. It's hard to think at all during cultural asphyxiation.

Do you feel this pressure? Under all the activity and demands and commuting, are you aware of the yoke around your neck?

Jesus was clear. We are all yoked to something. We are yoked to the pace of our culture, or we are yoked to him. We are learning his way of humility and ease, or we are learning the way of labor and burden. We are seeking first the kingdom of God or seeking first the kingdom of self (Matthew 6:33). You cannot serve two masters (verse 24). You cannot have two yokes, not without being torn apart.

I often wonder whether this is why the church lacks credibility in our world. Maybe it's not just our big scandals and cultural failures; maybe it's something much smaller, more common, more deadly. Maybe it's our exhaustion. Maybe we are just too tired to model *agapē* love, too scheduled to show compassion, too distracted to pray, too much like the exhausted culture around us.

OVERCOMING EXHAUSTION WITH SABBATH

I know of no more formative and countercultural practice for a culture of exhaustion than that of the Sabbath. In a 24-7 world, 24-6 living is a sign, wonder, and prophetic declaration that there is another way to live.

In the 1840s, urban life and pedestrian culture were beginning to flourish in Paris. The pace of life was quickening with industrialization. In protest against the violence of speed, a new prophetic pedestrian arose. The flaneur. The original flaneurs were known to stroll through the streets to reclaim their humanity. They would take turtles for walks like dogs and would let the turtle set the pace. Their use of time subverted the rising speed.

Practicing the Sabbath, in some ways, is a modern version of that for us. When we move through life at a sacred pace, creating time to pause and ponder and making space for God, it provokes questions about who and what is the functional lord of our lives.

There is tremendous confusion today as to the role the Sabbath is to play in our new-covenant lives. Some say that Jesus is our Sabbath rest and that observing part of the law makes us a slave to it all. Others argue that the Sabbath is a pre-law creational ordinance woven into the very fabric of creation. They point out it is the only command directly given to Adam and Eve by God.

But in our culture of burnout and exhaustion, perhaps we shouldn't be filtering this through simply a moral or doctrinal lens; perhaps we should be looking at it through a wisdom lens. Maybe God's six-to-one rhythm of creation and rest holds life and hope for our exhausted world. It seems that there is a grain to the universe that we live against at our own peril.

SABBATH AND TIME

Peter Scazzero, author of *Emotionally Healthy Spirituality*, said, "The word *Sabbath* comes from the Hebrew word that means 'to cease, to stop working.' It refers to doing nothing related to work for a twenty-four hour period each week. It refers to this unit of time around which we are to orient our entire lives as 'holy,' meaning 'separate' . . . [from] the other six days. . . . Sabbath provides for us now an additional rhythm for an entire reorientation of our lives around the living God."[8]

The call to Sabbath is found in Genesis, then reiterated throughout the Scriptures.

> The heavens and the earth were completed in all their vast array.
> By the seventh day God had finished the work he had been doing; so on the seventh day he rested from all his work. Then *God blessed the seventh day and made it holy,* because on it he rested from all the work of creating that he had done. (Genesis 2:1–3, emphasis added)

> Remember the Sabbath day by keeping it holy. Six days you shall labor and do all your work, but the seventh day is a sabbath to the LORD your God. On it you shall not do any work. (Exodus 20:8–10)

God laid out a vision of a twenty-four-hour period that is kept differently from the other days and is remembered as holy. It is a day that is blessed and given to an exhausted human race as a gift. Sabbath is given to us by God as a form of his grace and blessing, and our practice of the Sabbath is our gift to God of our trust, worship, and loyalty to his lordship in a culture of counterfeits.

In our society we have an unhealthy relationship to time. You can hear it in the way we talk: "Let me just say a prayer *real quick.*" "Hurry. We are going to be *late.*" "Time is *money.*" We are suffering from what Larry Dossey, an

American physician, called "time-sickness." He described an obsessive belief that "time is getting away, that there isn't enough of it, and that you must pedal faster and faster to keep up."[9] Carl Honoré noted, "The problem is that our love of speed, our obsession with doing more and more in less and less time, has gone too far; it has turned into an addiction, a kind of idolatry. Even when speed starts to backfire, we invoke the go-faster gospel. . . . Time-sickness can also be a symptom of a deeper, existential malaise. In the final stages before burnout, people often speed up to avoid confronting their unhappiness."[10]

The Sabbath allows us to reorient our relationship to time. Sabbath makes time, not place, holy. It is the reality of *kairos* time in a culture of *chronos*. Jewish theologian Abraham Joshua Heschel has written,

> Technical civilization . . . is man's triumph over space. Yet time remains impervious. We can overcome distance but can neither recapture the past nor dig out the future. Man transcends space, and time transcends man.
>
> Time is man's greatest challenge. . . . Space is exposed to our will; we may shape and change the things in space as we please. Time, however, is beyond our reach, beyond our power.[11]

In the twenty-four-hour period of Sabbath, we step out of the way of the world and into the way of eternity. We step into the space of the Spirit, of life, and of God. We step out of the space of the secular, of death, and of the prince of this age. Sabbath is a portal to participate in God's presence.

THE FOUR MOVEMENTS OF JESUS REST

Learning to practice the Sabbath requires that we are formed by repetition. There is no formation without repetition. We need a framework of Sabbath that makes Jesus's invitation to rest a reality in our lives. That framework follows four key movements: resist, rest, remember, revel.[12]

1. Resisting Work

Sabbath is marked not just by what we do but by what we abstain from. The center of this is ceasing from our work. Putting a boundary in place and stopping our work have tremendous spiritual, psychological, and emotional benefits. We remember that we are loved not for what we do but for who we are. We put our accomplishment and production down and allow God to be our provider and sustainer.

Marva Dawn wrote, "On the Sabbath day we deliberately remember that we have ceased trying to be God and instead have put our lives back into his control. Concentrating on God's Lordship in our lives enables us to return to his sovereign hands all the things that are beyond our control and terrifying us. Once those things are safely there, and as long as we don't stupidly take them back again, our emotions can find truly comforting and healing rest."[13]

We must learn to resist the insatiable desire to *do*. In this way, we resist defining our lives by our successes and failures. We refuse to believe we are what we do. We refuse to believe the world is sustained by our own power and effort. We resist the desire to control the outcomes of our lives. We no longer try to control people and use them for our own vision. We stop. We let go. We surrender.

Matitiahu Tsevat, a Hebrew scholar, said that the biblical Sabbath means an "acceptance of the sovereignty of God."[14] I am not trying to paint the picture here that work is fundamentally bad; in fact, it's a gift from God granted before the Fall, just as the Sabbath is. In the modern world, however, one of the central ways we engage in idolatry and independence is through our jobs.

We are just as prone to idolize protection and provision as the children of Israel were. Though they were concerned with crops, conception, and physical safety, they sought to control these areas by themselves. Their independence led to their downfall. When we practice the Sabbath, however, we declare our trust in and dependence on God. We confess with our lives that more recognition and more resources will not stave off disaster. God is our refuge and shield.

During Sabbath, we crawl under the shelter of his wings. From that vantage point, we stop our tireless thoughts. We put boundaries up for technology that draws us back into futile thought patterns, and we receive the gift of limits. The first movement of rest is resisting the tyranny of doing.

2. Resting and Restoration

We have an extraordinary need for rest today. Weariness seems to have taken over us all. Under the care of the Good Shepherd, our souls will be restored. Under the shepherding of our culture, our souls will be destroyed.

Our lack of rest carries serious health consequences. Research shows that "failing to rest after six days of steady work will lead to insomnia or sleepiness, hormonal imbalances, fatigue, irritability, organ stress, and other increasingly serious physical and mental symptoms."[15] But it is not just the physical or mental labor itself. Even turning our attention to matters of work when we are resting has been shown to trigger stress-induced anxiety. Thinking about work can be a form of work. This cycle of exhaustion must be addressed and broken through deep rest. Weariness rarely leads to godliness.

Two things must be challenged for rest to begin. The first trap is the mistaken idea that relaxation is the same thing as rest.

Many of us today are good at relaxing. We sit back with our fast food of choice and binge a few episodes or watch a game, and it does seem to work. Being drawn into a multi-episode, visually stimulating show can shift our minds away from the problems in our lives. Highly manufactured foods are designed to delight our taste buds, and highly manufactured entertainment can stir the emotions. But though these things may relax us, they rarely renew us.

Our souls are rarely restored through entertainment. Restoration comes through rest. Relaxation, though good, will not do a deep enough work.

The other trap that must be confronted is using the Sabbath merely as a day off. The day when we do all the chores and tasks we failed to do during our regular week because of the insanity of the pace of our lives. Tasks and chores are important and not going away anytime soon, but space should be given during the week for these. To bring them into the Sabbath is to pollute its purpose and rob us of rest. We shift from resisting to restoring not so there is more space for unfinished tasks but so there is time for soul-level recovery and rest.

The Sabbath is the gift of a weekly place for this restorative rest. Scholars have long pointed out the extraordinary phrase at the end of Exodus 31:17: "It will be a sign between me and the Israelites forever, for in six days the LORD made the heavens and the earth, *and on the seventh day he rested and was refreshed*" (emphasis added). Not only did God rest on the Sabbath; he was refreshed by it. The word *refreshed* means "to exhale," "catch one's breath," "breathe easy."[16] Let that sink in. If God rested on and was refreshed by the Sabbath, what power does it hold for us?

The movement from exhaustion to rest is a movement from fear to trust. A movement from anxiety to peace, a movement from control to surrender. But rest requires intentionality. We need to learn the skill of resting.

- We need *spiritual* rest. To stop our need to be on mission for God and do things for his kingdom. To stop our need to resist the culture around us and instead enjoy God's good gifts.
- We need *physical* rest. To sleep deeply, delight our senses, release stress, step back, and recover from the pace of modern life.
- We need *emotional* rest. To lower our guard and be ourselves before God. To lay down the concerns and conflicts of the week and be known and loved by him.
- We need *intellectual* rest. To stop having to deconstruct the lies and stories around us and instead feast on truth.
- We need *social* rest. To take a break from having to be "on" and give out to those around us. To enjoy acceptance and love from our Father and friends.

When we rest, we enable our whole beings to recover and reset the central pieces of our hearts and lives. If we are willing, he will give his beloved rest (Psalm 127:2).

3. Remembering Our True Identities

Perhaps there is no greater gift that the Sabbath brings us than the reminder and reformation of our true identities. We are terribly susceptible to the distortion of our identities in the modern workplace. We spend so much time there; how can it not shape us? As one business professor has noted, "Assuredly, other factors enter into the equation of self-identity—for example, genetic inheritance, race, gender, ethnicity, sexual orientation, religious training and family background. But even with all of these, work remains an irreducible given, the most common experience of adult life. The lessons we learn at work help formulate who we become and what we value as individuals and as a society. Whatever the conditions of our labor, work shapes us, and unfortunately, often malforms us."[17]

We spend a lot of time getting feedback on what we do at work, but rarely do we ask the question, Who are we becoming by what we are doing in our jobs? In a recent article in the *Atlantic* entitled "Workism Is Making Americans Miserable," author Derek Thompson addressed the way that work has come to shape our modern sense of self. He described this as a new kind of religion—workism.

> The economists of the early 20th century . . . failed to anticipate
> that . . . for the college-educated elite, [work] would morph into a
> kind of religion, promising identity, transcendence, and community.
> Call it workism. . . .
> . . . the belief that work is not only necessary to economic production, but also the centerpiece of one's identity and life's purpose; and the
> belief that any policy to promote human welfare must *always* encourage
> more work.

Atheism and the rise of the nones have shifted our sense of the transcendent from the divine to the doable. Thompson also wrote,

The decline of traditional faith in America has coincided with an
explosion of new atheisms. . . . And workism is among the most potent
of the new religions competing for congregants. . . .

One of the benefits of being an observant Christian, Muslim, or
Zoroastrian is that these God-fearing worshippers put their faith in an
intangible and unfalsifiable force of goodness. But work is tangible, and
success is often falsified. . . . To be a workist is to worship a god with
firing power.[18]

Sabbath is a chance to lay down the idol of workism, one of the idols we
looked at in the previous chapter, to resist the distortion of our identities, and
to experience a conversion of the heart. We must never doubt the power of Jesus
not only to save our souls but also to save our sense of self.

I have always empathized with the apostle John's desire to serve God. John
was called a "son of thunder" by Christ himself (Mark 3:17) and was always
at the center of the biblical action. He saw many of the insider miracles as one
of Jesus's three closest friends, and he was driven and passionate. You may remember him as the one asking Jesus whether he wanted him to call down fire
and destroy the village that rejected Christ (Luke 9:54). John was a son of
thunder.

Toward the end of Jesus's life, something began to shift in John's identity.
At a famous scene—the Last Supper when Jesus was sharing his new-covenant
vision and the horror of what was about to happen on the cross—chaos ensued.
A fight broke out as to which one of the disciples was the greatest (Luke 22:24);
Judas left the meal after agreeing to betray Jesus (John 13:30); Peter boasted
that he would never deny Jesus (Matthew 26:35). But where was the son of
thunder? In John 13, we read that he was reclining on Jesus's chest (verse 25).
He had the place of honor next to Jesus's heart.

From this moment, John's life was never quite the same. His identity seems
to have shifted. He transitioned from a son of thunder to the one Jesus loved.

He even had the cheek to write this in place of his name in his gospel. When you look at the rest of John's writings, you know why he is known as the apostle of love.

Secular slavery becomes spiritual sonship when we rest on Jesus's chest. On the Sabbath we embrace our God-given identity as children dearly loved by God. We don't have to achieve success, make a difference for God, or change the world. We simply enjoy being with him. We nurture our truest sense of identity and let the rest fall away. This weekly time with Jesus tempers our ungodly ambition and enables us to embrace who we really are. As A. J. Swoboda so beautifully said, "Sabbath is a scheduled weekly reminder that we are not what we do; rather, we are who we are loved by. Sabbath and the gospel scream the same thing: we do not work to get to a place where we finally get to breathe and rest—that is slavery. Rather, we rest and breathe and enjoy God *that we might* enter into rest."[19]

4. Reveling in God's Goodness

The final movement of the Sabbath is reveling. In a culture that seeks to numb us with senseless pleasure, we must recover the wonder of godly delight. Pastor John Ortberg said, "We must arrange life so that sin no longer looks good to us."[20] We often fall into the trap of believing that our faith is only about self-denial or asceticism, but the other side is a biblical delight in feasting on the goodness of God. On the Sabbath we are reminded that Christians are called to order desserts and laugh till it hurts.

Isaiah 25:6 paints this beautiful picture of what it's like to experience and enjoy God's salvation:

> On this mountain the LORD Almighty will prepare
>   a feast of rich food for all peoples,
> a banquet of aged wine—
>   the best of meats and the finest of wines.

One day a week, the shroud is lifted and we step into the beauty of eternity. The beauty where we taste the goodness of the age to come, the food and the wine and the worship, through the bounty of God's gifts of grace.

The Jewish philosopher Philo, a contemporary of Jesus, described the Sabbath day as "the birthday of the world" and "the festival, not of a single city or country, but of the universe."[21] I love that idea. Viewing the Sabbath as a festival of joy, a feast of God's favor. Two of the family's main duties on the Sabbath day, according to the rabbis, were to praise God and to enjoy food and drink in the home. To gather round the table and listen and laugh and enjoy. If we are married, we are called to feast on the gift of sexuality. To explore and remind each other of the gift of physical pleasure and love. We are called to feast on beauty. To fill our hearts with painting and photography and poetry and literature and nature. We are called to feast on friendship. To enjoy the company of friends and family and drink deeply from the well of belonging. We are called to feast on God, to again "taste and see that the LORD is good" (Psalm 34:8).

I believe in the concept of pleasure stacking on the Sabbath. While we ate a Shabbat meal in Jerusalem with some Jewish hosts, they told about the special foods and treats they save to make the day even sweeter. The Sabbath is filled with sensory delight and wonder that remind us, if even for a moment, that Jesus is making all things new (Revelation 21:5).

SAVING YOUR LIFE

As a young leader, I ached for development and formation, so I devoured books and conferences on leadership and growth. Over time I began to notice a trend. Every conference had the same talk in it; every book had the same chapter in it. It was about burnout. Everyone on the stage and page seemed to follow the same path. They worked like mad to pursue their visions; they burned out and harmed their families, friends, and themselves. Then they slowed their pace and changed their rhythms. They all urged people to learn from their mistakes and build rest into the framework of their lives.

At one point I thought, *I am the biblical definition of a fool if I don't do this*. So I resolved in my early twenties that I would practice a weekly rhythm of Sabbath as a part of my leadership and life. Though we haven't done so perfectly, it's one thing we have done well over the years. My wife and I have had to work at times to juggle kids' sports, travel, leadership crises, health emergencies, and financial strain, but it has been worth it. This stubborn resistance to letting the culture crush us with its pace and power has kept our hearts alive and enabled us to live at a sacred pace, with the balance of urgency and sustainability that displays a provocative faith to a withering world.

"Sabbath cannot save your soul, but it very well may save your life," wrote Swoboda.[22] And a movement of rest has begun. In the middle of New York, I see a new kind of disciple rising. Those who know that work is a gift but not a god and that more money and praise don't add to the bottom line of their worth before God. God is raising up people who live at a sacred pace, who value formation as much as fame, relationships as much as recognition, and abiding over outcomes. Those who are deadly serious about learning Jesus's way of rest. Those who have refused the relentless rhythm of the culture and live for him alone. These are the people who don't want to spend the first half of their lives abusing themselves and the second half trying to make amends. Those who cultivate the fourth kind of soil and are enjoying its fruit (Matthew 13:23).

May the same be true of us. May Jesus teach us not just to pray, disciple, care for the poor, confront hypocrisy, fast, cast out demons, and worship the one true God. May we take him up on his invitation to learn from his humble heart. May you learn that rest can resist exhaustion.

Hunger Must Resist Apathy

> Man shall not live on bread alone.
>
> Matthew 4:4

> [Fasting] is a desperate measure, for desperate times, among those who know themselves desperate for God.
>
> DAVID MATHIS, "Sharpen Your Affections with Fasting"

> Fasting in the biblical sense is choosing not to partake of food because your spiritual hunger is so deep, your determination in intercession so intense, or your spiritual warfare so demanding that you have temporarily set aside even fleshly needs to give yourself to prayer and meditation.
>
> WESLEY L. DUEWEL, *Touch the World Through Prayer*

A crowd had gathered, and things were getting tense. A young boy with a demon had been brought to Jesus's disciples for them to cast it out. The disciples had had some success in this kind of thing before. They tried, but nothing seemed to happen. They tried again, and the boy gnashed his teeth and passed out. The intensity increased. Nothing that had worked for them before seemed to matter in this moment. Try as they would, the demon wouldn't come out. The boy remained in torment and bondage.

So they did what people without power always seem to do: they broke into a theological dispute. Ideas and theology emerged to explain their lack of power. The teachers of the law started sharing their theories, and the conflict escalated. Meanwhile, the boy was in torment and the father in anguish.

Enter Jesus. He had been on the Mount of Transfiguration and now rejoined his disciples.

When the demon saw him, it convulsed the boy and threw him to the ground. After Jesus exhorted the father to have faith, rebuked the demon, and drove it out, it was time for a ministry debrief. And it was here that Jesus peeled the curtain back on the operations of the supernatural. In Mark 9:28–29, we encounter the scene:

> When He had come into the house, His disciples asked Him privately, "Why could we not cast it out?"
>
> So He said to them, "This kind can come out by nothing but prayer and fasting." (NKJV)

This was a power contest we should be able to recognize.

The church faces a multitude of obstacles and enemies as she pursues her mission today. And you face many in your own life. So many powers, ideologies, and systems seem to be set up against the things of God. As a result, we are hemorrhaging young people from the church; many churches are in numerical decline; faith seems as if it exists on the wrong side of history. At the same time, we have more theological resources than ever before, more understanding of the roots of our problems, more conferences and training, billions of dollars flowing through church programs, yet very little seems to change. The things we have historically done to see the world renewed seem to have no power. And like the disciples and the teachers of the law, we have turned to disputes and theories. We have formed coalitions and alliances and networks. Meanwhile, decline accelerates. The powers that hold the world in bondage refuse to give. "This kind"—the things our generation, and you personally, are wrestling with—will not come out with normal methods. What we have done in the past won't work in the future of the church. This kind won't go quietly.

It can be incredibly demoralizing to live in a time of decline. It's heavy. These forces seem to come from so many directions, and resistance seems so hard that many eventually capitulate. Many just give up, make peace with the present, and get through the best they can. Others turn inward and look at sensational events and Christian trends and believe all is fine. Others lose interest in the things of God and settle for a mediocre faith. This happened to the church in Laodicea: "You say, 'I am rich; I have acquired wealth and do not need a thing.' But you do not realize that you are wretched, pitiful, poor, blind and naked" (Revelation 3:17). This body is the one that Christ said was "lukewarm—neither hot nor cold" and thus he would spit them out of his mouth (verse 16). This lukewarmness results in a spiritual numbness and disregard for what we face.

What will it take to see change? How will we move beyond debates and into powerful encounter? How can we shift from ideas to authority? Something has to snap us out of it. As C. S. Lewis put it, "You and I have need of the strongest spell that can be found to wake us from the evil enchantment of worldliness."[1]

Jesus's statement to the disciples was a startling revelation. There were certain things that wouldn't change without fasting and prayer. The disciples were up against something that required a new level of desperation and power. They were going to have to press in through prayer and fasting.

Now, when you read this, you may have an immediate reaction. *Prayer is hard but doable . . . but fasting? That's horrible and impossible.*

My initial reaction is the same. Is there any other way than this somber discipline? It's easier to discuss ideas than contend for change. Easier to look at my own life and own problems and muddle my way through and let someone else press in.

But before we know it, each of us will face circumstances where our ideas and opinions will fall short. What we have relied on will let us down. We will all have moments like the father in Mark 9 when we will need help for ourselves and those we love. Where can we turn then? These words of Jesus will hit us with fresh impact. *This kind,* the struggle in front of us, will require us to shake off our apathy and numbness and seek him with desperation as we never have before. We will turn to prayer and fasting, for they resist apathy.

CONFRONTING OUR SPIRITUAL NUMBNESS

We live in a culture infatuated with food. So much of our vision of the good life is infused with epicurean delight. Almost every image of joy we hold is centered on a table. For the Romans, the good life was reclining on couches surrounded by bones and olive pits. Today Instagram food shots, dozens of food shows, and celebrity chefs emphasize food unlike at any other time in history. It seems food has come to dominate every facet of our existence.

In New York, we have an entire street dedicated to the creation and consumption of food—Restaurant Row in Hell's Kitchen. I live one block from there. If they gave out awards for attendance, I would have a gold star.

In the book *A Framework for Understanding Poverty,* Ruby Payne helped the reader understand how the poor, the middle class, and the wealthy have come to view different categories of life. It's a profoundly insightful explanation of social stratification. The section on food perspectives has always stood out to me.

- For the poor the key question is about quantity: *Did I have enough?*
- For the middle class the key question is about quality: *Did I like it?*
- For the wealthy the key question is about presentation: *Was it aesthetically pleasing?*[2]

These perspectives in some ways work to make food central at every level of society. Fast food consumes and harms the poor; the middle class obsess over quality and sourcing; and the wealthy spend obscene amounts in pursuit of the perfect plate. Food is an obsession for us all.

Now, there certainly comes a time for feasting, as I will emphasize in the upcoming chapter on celebration. But there is also a time for fasting. Many times, in fact. And if you're like most people in the food-obsessed West, fasting is not so easy.

One day into a fast—maybe even one meal in—you will become acutely aware of the role food plays in your life. Spiritual formation theologian Richard Foster noted, "More than any other Discipline, fasting reveals the things that control us. . . . We cover up what is inside us with food and other good things."[3] There are many good things that we are allowed to partake of as recipients of God's grace in all its forms, but at times these gifts move into the categories of entitlement and addiction. They begin to become our default understanding of discipleship in a Western context. We binge-watch entire television shows without thought, consider wine essential at any real celebration, and spend disproportionate amounts of money on eating out compared with disciples of Jesus in almost any other part of the world. All these things slowly numb our spiritual senses in our walk with God.

Pastor John Piper, commenting on the power of Western culture, wrote,

> Jesus said some people hear the word of God, and a desire for God is awakened in their hearts. But then, "as they go on their way they are choked by the cares and riches and *pleasures of life*" (Luke 8:14). In another place he said, "*The desires for other things* enter in and choke the word, and it proves unfruitful" (Mark 4:19). "The pleasures of life" and "the desires for other things"—these are not evil in themselves. These are not vices. These are gifts of God. They are your basic meat and potatoes and coffee and gardening and reading and decorating and traveling and investing and TV-watching and Internet-surfing and shopping and exercising and collecting and talking. And all of them can become deadly substitutes for God. . . .
>
> The greatest enemy of hunger for God is not poison but apple pie. It is not the banquet of the wicked that dulls our appetite for heaven,

but endless nibbling at the table of the world. It is not the X-rated
video, but the prime-time dribble of triviality we drink in every night.[4]

Fasting is spiritual resistance against Western cultural numbness. But
what does it actually look like when we do it?

WHAT IS FASTING?

Despite all the confusion around fasting, as a practice it is quite simple. Biblical
fasting is refraining from food for a spiritual purpose. There is the *absolute fast,*
where water and food are given up completely for a short time. If you tried this
today, you would probably require medical intervention fairly quickly. We see
this occasionally in Scripture during the direst of circumstances. There is what
theologians call the *normal fast,* which is what most of us think of when we
think of fasting—you still drink to take in liquids, but you stop eating and
turn your energies toward prayer and intercession, toward the reading of Scripture and other spiritual activities. Finally, there's the *partial fast.* We see this in
the book of Daniel, when Daniel chose to refrain from particular categories of
food, still receiving sustenance but rejecting any food that gave him joy (10:3).

Fasting is designed to shift our focus from our bodies to our spirits and
from our flesh to our Father. The goal is to enter into deeper communion with
him. It is marked by intentionality in our withdrawal from food. Pastor Jentezen Franklin noted the importance of this focus: "Whenever you begin a fast,
remember, if it doesn't mean anything to you, it won't mean anything to God.
Without being combined with prayer and the Word, fasting is little more than
dieting."[5]

In today's food-oriented context, people are always trying to fast from everything except food. We say things like "fasting from social media," "fasting
from criticizing others," "fasting from purchasing clothes." As good and important as these things are, I don't believe they fall into the same category as biblical fasting. They may be useful practices and focuses, but fasting seems to be

tied to food. (I do believe there is an exception for those who struggle with eating disorders.)[6] It is replacing physical sustenance with spiritual sustenance. Fasting is designed to reveal our dependence, not just tweak our habits.

KING STOMACH

When you look back over redemptive history, it is remarkable how much spiritual danger and disobedience were related to the simple comforts of food.[7] Adam and Eve were tempted in part by the appearance of the food laid in front of them by the Enemy. Genesis 3:6 reads, "When the woman saw that the fruit of the tree was good for food and pleasing to the eye, and also desirable for gaining wisdom, she took some and ate it. She also gave some to her husband, who was with her, and he ate it." Esau was willing to give up his birthright for a pot of stew in a moment of hunger. "See that no one is sexually immoral, or is godless like Esau, who for a single meal sold his inheritance rights as the oldest son. Afterward, as you know, when he wanted to inherit this blessing, he was rejected. Even though he sought the blessing with tears, he could not change what he had done" (Hebrews 12:16–17).

The children of Israel shrank back from their destiny of deliverance when they remembered the food of Egypt. Numbers 11:4–6 records, "The rabble with them began to crave other food, and again the Israelites started wailing and said, 'If only we had meat to eat! We remember the fish we ate in Egypt at no cost—also the cucumbers, melons, leeks, onions and garlic. But now we have lost our appetite; we never see anything but this manna!'" At no cost? They were slaves for four hundred years, yet the desire for food distorted their memories and sowed the seeds of disobedience.

In *The Lion, the Witch and the Wardrobe*, C. S. Lewis painted a powerful portrait of King Stomach at work. Edmund, after being transported to Narnia, has an encounter with the White Witch, the Queen who is holding Narnia captive. When she realizes who Edmund is—a boy, a son of Adam, a human—she appeals to a fundamental weakness. Gently coaxing him, she says,

"It is dull, Son of Adam, to drink without eating. . . . What would you like best to eat?"

"Turkish Delight, please, your Majesty," said Edmund. . . .

While he was eating the Queen kept asking him questions. At first Edmund tried to remember that it is rude to speak with one's mouth full, but soon he forgot about this and thought only of trying to shovel down as much Turkish Delight as he could, and the more he ate the more he wanted to eat, and he never asked himself why the Queen should be so inquisitive. . . .

At last the Turkish Delight was all finished and Edmund was looking very hard at the empty box and wishing that she would ask him whether he would like some more. Probably the Queen knew quite well what he was thinking; for she knew, though Edmund did not, that this was enchanted Turkish Delight and that anyone who had once tasted it would want more and more of it, and would even, if they were allowed, go on eating it till they killed themselves.[8]

Serving King Stomach can cause incredible compromise and weaken the church. Comfort can blind us to the powerlessness we have compared with the purposes and promises of God. It can create an insatiable appetite for the flesh and the world. We settle for so much less than God has for us. I remember once asking a believer in the persecuted church what he thought of the American church. His response has stuck with me for years: "So much food, so little power."

CHANGING AN EMPIRE

On September 20, 1932, Gandhi gently laid his plate aside and, with intentionality and defiance, decided it was time to fast. Again. The British government was supporting a new constitution in India that would divide the electorate, separating the "untouchable" caste and causing them to have their own seats in the government. This might sound like a good thing to the uninitiated, but Gandhi believed that a divided India would not last, nor would it be just for all Indian people, so he stopped eating as a way of protesting the decision handed down by the seemingly unstoppable British Empire.

This was not the first fast Gandhi had undertaken during India's freedom movement. In fact, Gandhi undertook seventeen fasts, ranging from one to twenty-one days, as a way of striving for unity and disarming the unjust power structures that existed in India during his lifetime. Fasting became a kind of peaceful weapon for Gandhi, and several of his longest fasts were undertaken as a kind of striving for Hindu-Muslim unity and improved conditions for the "untouchable" caste.

Six days after Gandhi began his fast in 1932, the British government withdrew the offending constitutional clauses. One man—physically unimposing, owning no weapons, and directing no army—had caused the most powerful empire on earth to change course.

This was a typical result when Gandhi would fast—he rarely undertook a fast without gaining the outcome he was advocating for. He was so widely beloved in India during that time that as soon as he announced he was fasting, the entire country held its breath. People stopped going to work. Rioting and fighting between Muslims and Hindus ceased as the populace turned their attention to this tiny warrior. They prayed for him in their temples and mosques. Pressure on the government increased. Fasting, Gandhi proved, can be a powerful force. Fasting is a tool of radical resistance against an empire.

THE CENTRALITY OF FASTING

Throughout history, fasting has been an important practice in both religious tradition and political defiance. Muslims fast during Ramadan, abstaining from food for thirty days during sunlight hours. Hindu practitioners fast during set days and seasons; the Jewish community fasts on days like Yom Kippur and Purim. There is also a resurgence of fasting in mainstream society; however, it is often separated from a religious framework. Fasting is not seen as a tool of self-denial, the redirection of desire, or a means to deeper prayer. Rather than aiding the formation of the soul, modern fasting is seen as a tool for physical transformation. The keto diet is a fast from carbs, intermittent fasting rests our guts and resets our metabolism, and juice fasting cleanses toxins from our bodies.

The Christian tradition also has a rich history of fasting. In the Catholic Church, people fourteen years of age and older are required to abstain from eating meat on Fridays in honor of Jesus's suffering and death on Good Friday. The forty days of Lent are also considered a time for fasting. Anglican and Orthodox believers have a liturgical framework for fasting, building self-denial into their yearly rhythms. Occasionally, fasting trends run through the larger Christian church, such as the Daniel Diet and twenty-one-day breakthrough fasts.

Even though there are historical precedent and evangelical fads, in over two decades of pastoral experience, I have rarely met a Christian for whom fasting is a central part of discipleship and formation. Would Jesus really believe fasting is important in our world of food selfies and celebrity chefs?

In Luke 4, Jesus faced the same primal temptation as Adam, yet Jesus had a deeper hunger and resisted the temptation food brought. Verses 1–4 record this encounter:

> Jesus, full of the Holy Spirit, left the Jordan and was led by the Spirit into the wilderness, where for forty days he was tempted by the devil. He ate nothing during those days, and at the end of them he was hungry.
>
> The devil said to him, "If you are the Son of God, tell this stone to become bread."
>
> Jesus answered, "It is written: 'Man shall not live on bread alone.'"

Jesus knew the truth about desire and satisfaction. Jesus valued obedience and intimacy over satiation. His deeper desire to please the Father overrode his lesser desire to eat. In a later passage Jesus said that his food was to do the will of his Father (John 4:34). Fasting reinforces our true desires and reorients us to the presence of God. Fasting can dethrone King Stomach and lead us into a space where we can examine and reorder our desires.

This is illustrated powerfully throughout the New Testament and especially in Paul's letters where he contrasted the spirit and the flesh. As Christians, we believe that the body is a gift from God, and everything the body does can be used for the glory of God. Sex, eating, and physical activity—all are gifts God has given us. But we also have to guard against being driven by inordinate desires that come out of these gifts.

Most of our culture is not engaged in a nuanced evaluation of desire. Instead, our culture is mostly driven by two questions: *How do I feel? What do I want?* These are the mechanisms that drive twenty-first-century civilization. Fasting is one of God's great tools for reorienting our longings away from the flesh and back toward God. All of us have deeply engraved patterns, dopamine-reward mechanisms, and neural pathways centered around a need for physical satisfaction. Fasting breaks these default connections and reorients us toward a greater food: intimacy with and enjoyment of God.

DELIGHTING IN THE LORD

"Fasting from any nourishment, activity, involvement, or pursuit—for any season—sets the stage for God to appear," wrote Dan Allender. "Fasting is not a tool to pry wisdom out of God's hands or to force needed insight about a decision. Fasting is not a tool for gaining discipline or developing piety (whatever that might be). Instead, fasting is the bulimic act of ridding ourselves of our fullness to attune our senses to the mysteries that swirl in and around us."[9] *Setting the stage for God.* I love that. Don't you want him to play a larger role in your story? Fasting creates the place for that.

Once, while I was on an extended fast, the voice of the Lord became so clear and easy for me to understand. The signal through the noise was startling. God revealed several areas of disobedience that had been hiding under excuses, and hard-to-discern idols came into clear focus. He provided such intimacy with his heart that I almost couldn't take it. His love was so present and powerful that I wanted to fast for the rest of my life. I was beginning to taste the hidden manna of which Jesus spoke (Revelation 2:17), the food of which the world knows nothing about.

Jentezen Franklin wrote, "There are dimensions of our glorious King that will never be revealed to the casual, disinterested worshiper. There are walls of intercession that will never be scaled by dispassionate religious service. But when you take steps to break out of the ordinary and worship Him as He deserves, you will begin to see facets of His being you never knew existed. He will begin to share secrets with you about Himself, His plans, His desires for you. When you worship God as He deserves, He is magnified."[10]

Anna understood this reality. Her story is recorded in Luke 2:36–37: "There was also a prophet, Anna, the daughter of Penuel, of the tribe of Asher. She was very old; she had lived with her husband seven years after her marriage, and then was a widow until she was eighty-four. She never left the temple but worshiped night and day, fasting and praying." Anna gave her life to prayer and fasting, and what was the result? She was one of the few in her generation given the privilege of seeing the Messiah. Fasting tuned her in to the secrets of God, secrets few others were able to hear.

God also grants intimacy and insight to churches that fast to seek his guidance. In Acts 13:2–3, the early church was seeking direction for apostolic mission. While the Christians at Antioch were worshipping and fasting, God broke in and gave them direction and anointing for the mission that would take the gospel to the ends of the earth. Corporate fasting is one of the most strategic ways we can move away from human-centered leadership and decision-making and accelerate kingdom mission in our time.

Fasting for Breakthrough

In Joel 2, God laid out his plan of judgment before the people, highlighting the terror that would come in light of his wrath. Yet in the midst of the warning, God made an appeal to his people. Verses 15–17 say,

> Blow the trumpet in Zion,
>> declare a holy fast,
>> call a sacred assembly.
> Gather the people,
>> consecrate the assembly. . . .
> Let them say, "Spare your people, LORD.
>> Do not make your inheritance an object of scorn,
>> a byword among the nations."

And what was the purpose of this holy fast, this crying out? Verses 13–14 tell us:

> Return to the LORD your God,
>> for he is gracious and compassionate,
> slow to anger and abounding in love,
>> and he relents from sending calamity.
> Who knows? He may turn and relent
>> and leave behind a blessing.

Fasting can turn back judgment and unleash blessing in its place. God calls the whole community to utilize this tool.

I recently encountered the power of fasting and sacred assemblies while visiting a friend who was a part of a 24-7 prayer room in Atlanta. "What do you see God doing right now?" I asked her during my visit.

"You've actually come at a really good time," she explained. "We are in the middle of a forty-day fast because we have a sense that God wants to break the spirit of racism in Atlanta." I was amazed—and a little taken aback. What an approach! I'm sure there were people petitioning the government and working on court cases and trying to create laws that addressed this problem—necessary and important work—but here was a group of people who had decided that the way to bring about change was to fast, to contend alongside God for tangible change in their city.

"For a couple of years," she continued, "a group of African American pastors has come together with white pastors in Atlanta, working through reconciliation. A well-known prophetic leader in the city gave a word that God wanted to break the spirit of racism in Atlanta, and this group of pastors took this word seriously."

This movement, OneRace, has brought together 560 pastors. They hosted a summit on top of Stone Mountain, Georgia, one of the central, historical locations of the KKK. It also happens to have the largest Confederate monument in the country, etched into the side of a cliff. The meeting at Stone Mountain was the climax of their prayer and fasting.

In an article by *Christianity Today* about this event, Billy Humphrey, cofounder of OneRace, said, "The Lord wants to eradicate racism and dead religion in every form in the church. He wants to expose blind spots of prejudice, privilege, bitterness, and fear. The answer to division and hate is the gospel of Jesus Christ." And Jonathan Tremaine Thomas, a young pastor from Ferguson, Missouri, said, "Heaven is among us. The kingdom of heaven is at hand."

The article went on to say that "Thomas was followed by civil rights leader John Perkins, who was followed by apologies from Christian leaders to two Jewish leaders for the history of Christian anti-Semitism, who were followed by declarations of forgiveness for Dylann Roof by family members of Charleston church shooting victims."[11]

More than three thousand people showed up at the monument for this celebration of forgiveness and racial reconciliation, and it received the attention of other cities around the world that started to ask, "How can we see that kind of movement in our own communities?"

This is what our nation needs. This is what the church needs. And it was all put into motion by prayer and fasting.

So many of us today are heartbroken by the state of our nation and the collective sense of despair. Frustration is boiling over. Some people resign their hope, others stage protests, but it all eventually goes back to normal. The anger and the upheaval rarely lead to significant change. We keep trying the same things, and we keep getting the same tired results. But what if? What if the people of God seized on the things that need to be changed—the injustice and the exploitation and the corruption—and, instead of lobbying a politician or creating a new petition, they went before the God of the universe, the God who has all power and authority, the God who can break in and change the game? What would happen if the people of God directly petitioned God through fasting?

Historically, when God's people have turned to him through fasting, he breaks in and brings radical change.

- Moses's forty-day fast resulted in the revelation of the Ten Commandments (Exodus 34:28).
- Hannah fasted, and God released a prophet who changed the destiny of a nation (1 Samuel 1:7–20).
- Esther called for a fast, and her people were delivered and their enemies routed (Esther 4:16; 7:3–9:16).
- Jesus fasted for forty days in the wilderness and overcame the temptations that held humanity in bondage (Luke 4:1–13).

We have tried every other type of solution. Maybe "this kind" will come out only through prayer and fasting.

BEGIN AGAIN WITH FASTING

Following Jesus in our Western world can sometimes feel exhausting. Secularism, cynicism, immorality, and injustice can make us feel as if we are already paying a price to be faithful to Jesus. Isn't it enough to just live without compromise? Yet we are called to do more than survive; we are called to seek first God's kingdom (Matthew 6:33), believing that God can and will move in response to the cries of his people. Hunger must be stronger than our culturally induced apathy.

In Elie Wiesel's *Night,* the Holocaust survivor recounted an anecdote about people discussing whether to fast on Yom Kippur in a concentration camp. Wiesel wrote, "The Day of Atonement. Should we fast? The question was hotly debated. . . . In this place, we were always fasting. It was Yom Kippur year-round. But there were those who said we should fast, precisely because it was dangerous to do so. We needed to show God that even here, locked in hell, we were capable of singing His praises."[12] This spirit of defiance has always marked God's people. God has given us a way to transcend our experiences and call on his name.

At the starting point of Jesus's ministry, after he was baptized by John and identified by God as his Son (Luke 3:21–22), Jesus could have gone out and done many things. But he didn't mark that momentous occasion by hosting a huge celebration or holding a press conference or preaching to thousands on a hillside. He didn't garner attention with a spectacular healing or enter the city of Jerusalem with fanfare. Jesus marked the beginning of his ministry by engaging in a forty-day fast.

What does this say about where we should begin? What if, before we undertook major initiatives, we followed Jesus's example? What if we fasted, sought God's heart, and submitted our plans to him?

At the end of the forty-day fast, we read in Luke's gospel, Jesus was hungry, and this is when the Enemy came to tempt him, at what seemed his weakest point. His physical longings for food had peaked, he was feeling weak, yet what did he do in that moment? Jesus resisted the Enemy (4:1–13).

In Genesis, we see Adam getting this all wrong. He was surrounded by food and provision, yet he was tempted by the Enemy and gave in to the temptation of food (3:1–6). But here we see Jesus, the second Adam, experience a completely different outcome. Jesus was outwardly weak and physically hungry, yes, but fasting had strengthened his spirit. Inwardly, Jesus was being renewed with power. This is what fasting will do. It strengthens our spirits. It reorders our loves and allows us to feast on the goodness of God, enabling breakthroughs and a new level of self-control in our lives. Fasting increases our intimacy with—and delight in—God.

BRINGING BACK A PRODIGAL

Like the gospel story of a son with a demon, I know another story of a troubled son. One tormented by rebellion and recklessness and rage. One who could not be controlled and caused heartache to those around him. His father turned to the traditional church and the theologies of his day, but nothing seemed to change. The son's rebellion increased. Yet the father remembered this scene from Jesus's life. He remembered that some things wouldn't come out without prayer and fasting. So he set his heart to seek God for his son. He pressed in— set his alarm, fasted, and cried out for the prodigal's return.

Over a period of about six months, something began to change. The son's heart was rescued from rebellion and drawn to love. He was swept into the kingdom of God, and everything his father had fasted and prayed for happened. The son went on to become a pastor and missionary to another nation.

That father was my father. I am that son.

Through our fasting, God can bring home the prodigal, break through resistance, open the heavens, transform the darkest situation. There is so much at stake; I urge you—let your hunger resist your apathy.

Chapter 5

Hospitality Must Resist Fear

Our biggest fear may turn out to be our greatest opportunity.

KRISH KANDIAH, *God Is Stranger*

Do not forget to show hospitality to strangers, for by so doing some people have shown hospitality to angels without knowing it.

Hebrews 13:2

In November 2008, dozens of prominent white nationalists gathered in a hotel in Memphis to plan how to respond to a national crisis: Americans had just elected their first black president.

Although leading figures in the white supremacy movement from the United States, Canada, and Russia filled the room, the star of the show was a college student from Florida who had recently turned nineteen. Derek Black, known as "the heir," was the son of Don Black, the creator of Stormfront, the largest white nationalist website in the world. At one point Derek's mother had been married to David Duke, former grand wizard of the KKK. Duke had organized the Memphis meeting. When Derek's turn came to speak, he cast a vision about how politics could become an avenue to take the movement mainstream.

Rather than playing Ultimate Frisbee, watching Netflix, or taking sociology classes on white privilege, Derek had given his life to the purity and protection of the white race. Keeping his identity secret from his friends, he would sneak out of his dorm to call in to his radio program. Young, smart, socially aware, and politically active, a young man like Derek certainly could be "the heir" of white supremacist America.[1]

How does a nineteen-year-old student get swept up into such a hate-filled ideology? How does such disdain and intolerance take over a young man's heart? How? Fear. Fear of the other. Fear of change, fear of loss, fear of the unknown. The same fears that cause us to prioritize our lives over others'.

We live in a moment when we are facing relational and social change at dizzying rates. Life used to be comfortable for most people, designed to reflect their values and preferences. People gathered by race, class, religion, and shared moral frameworks. There is a psychological ease in being surrounded by similar people. Outsiders were kept at a safe distance, the occasional encounter driving us deeper into safe community. But with the arrival of the internet, ease of travel, apps that connect us to people around the world, shifts in political power, and college campuses becoming more diverse, a new generation has arisen that values equality and diversity over sameness. In many ways this new diversity has been seen as a threat, and threats stir anxiety and fear.

Yet what if we—the followers of Jesus—were to act more like him by being the ones to reach out to people who are different from us? What if we gathered with strangers to share simple human pleasures, such as meals? What if we got to know others and let them know us? It wouldn't erase the differences, but it just might cancel the fear. It just might help us overcome some of the divisions and isolation in our society. It just might enable us to show Jesus to people in a way that they would never otherwise encounter him. Others might begin to follow our lead. The future might be one of inclusion and belonging.

But first, hospitality must resist fear.

THE OTHER

The philosopher Hegel was the first to use the term "the other,"[2] but it has come to be used primarily in sociological contexts as the way that majority and minority social identities are constructed.

There are different kinds of "other." Our society values the exotic other, someone different from us but from a socially approved or desirable position. I sometimes experience this, being from Australia. I've never met anyone who has questioned my presence in the United States. People almost always excitedly tell me that they love Australia and have always hoped to visit. Even though I am an immigrant, an "other," I am not categorized as an immigrant in the same sense as those from Central America or Muslim countries. I am not *that* kind of other. My otherness is exotic, in stark contrast to the "undesirable other" of whom we are afraid. That one we keep at a distance. Fear of this kind of other is what drives so much of our political and religious dialogue today.

Categorizing people as *other* has a profound impact on our capacity to love. It changes our desire for connection and the responsibility we feel. Distance creates fear, and fear gives us a hermeneutic of suspicion, causing us to withhold care. Harvard psychologist Mina Cikara said that when you start fearing others, "your circle of who you counted as friends is going to shrink. And that means those people outside of the bounds get less empathy, get fewer resources."[3]

Theologian Miroslav Volf suggested that our entire culture has been built on "the persistent practice of exclusion."[4] This practice means that our instincts are continually sharpened to push others to the margins of our minds, hearts, and lives. Rather than being seen as a gift, others are seen as a threat to the sameness and security we expect.

Andrew Shepherd, a teacher of theology and ethics, said,

> Building relationships with the stranger has become increasingly difficult in an age where the dual discourses of the "war on terror"

and "the market" hold sway. The influence of these pervasive discourses means Others come to be conceived as threats. The stranger is either to be explicitly feared—a potential "terrorist" coming to "destroy civilization" and our place in it—or, is simply another abstract commodity, at best, to be "tolerated," or at worst, competing for limited resources, one to be struggled against.[5]

Shepherd detailed this process of exclusion. First, we seek to *eliminate* unwanted others from our circle of life, either through legislation or violence. If we can't remove them, we seek to *assimilate* others, to make them like ourselves so that we don't have to live with undesired difference. If that doesn't work, we seek to *dominate* others, to normalize our own standards and penalize for variance, and if that doesn't work, we turn to *demonization*.[6] We remove their humanity to justify any behavior.

A culture that has removed the supernatural from its thinking will not do away with the concepts of the supernatural; it will transfer them to the natural. Without acknowledging actual fallen angels and enemies of God, we turn others into fallen members of our desired social conditions and enemies of ourselves. Christians with a Satan-less gospel will project the anger that should be reserved for Lucifer onto other social groups, ignoring the apostle Paul's reminder that we fight not against flesh and blood but against principalities and powers (Ephesians 6:12). When the church takes her cues from culture and eliminates, assimilates, dominates, and demonizes image bearers of God, she bears no resemblance to Jesus Christ, whose compassion defied all social categories and was defined by deep embrace. Demonization leads to dehumanization.

I have a friend who pastors a megachurch in a beautiful part of the country. The church is in one of the most beautiful parts of that city. It has a desirable school district, an Apple Store at its local mall, and Coldplay in the speakers of the high-end gyms. It is the life that many long for.

Yet in the middle of the peace and prosperity, my friend's heart began to change. He began to get a vision for the rest of the city. God began to lift his eyes beyond the borders of his comfortable life. He began to care about the forgotten and undesirable places, those that others avoid or leave. He began to look at the immigrants and outsiders, those excluded from the life he enjoyed.

So he shared his heart with the congregation to raise money for a new work in these other parts of town. They wanted to strengthen those already faithfully serving the community in deep incarnational love. He wasn't trying to parachute in as a colonizing savior of the poor; he was seeking to share what they had with those they had ignored. He cast a vision for a special offering and called the members of his congregation to open their hearts in love.

I called him to see how it went. To my surprise, there was despondency in his voice. In general, people gave money and a round of applause, but he was shaken by something else. Fear. One comment dealt a blow to his heart: "Those illegals are taking American jobs."

Seek first the kingdom of America, said Jesus never. Eliminate, assimilate, dominate, and demonize.

I understand that nuance is required in this vast and complex discussion of the other. I understand shifting morality, a world of nation-states, the rule of law, responsibility to family and local community, and the loss of secure futures. But I also understand the teaching of Scripture and the call for the people of God to open their hearts out of loyalty to Christ. My deep concern is that our current political and social debates—not only about immigration but also about much else—are happening among Christians without a biblical understanding of these areas. As a result, the voice of Jesus is being drowned out by the cacophony of fear.

Christine Pohl, professor emeritus of ethics, addressed this: "Even among Christians, many of the current discussions about poverty and welfare, inclusion and diversity, scarcity and distribution, are conducted without the benefit of any coherent theological framework. Often, the result is that our stands on complex social and public policy concerns are little affected by our deepest

Christian values and commitments. Hospitality as a framework provides a bridge which connects our theology with daily life and concerns."[7] A theology of hospitality can rekindle love and cast out fear.

GOD'S LOVE OF THE STRANGER

The Greek word for "hospitality" is beautiful: *philoxenia*. It is a compound combining *philos* (a word meaning "friend" that is related to *phileo,* the verb for nonerotic love) and *xenos* ("foreigner"). Rather than fear of the other, hospitality is love for the other.

The reason God calls us to this kind of love is that this is the way he has loved us.

We often forget what our lives were like before God saved us. We project ourselves into the story of salvation in distorted ways, misreading Scripture as though we were the insider group. We read as if Jesus came to reaffirm our belonging and acceptance. But nothing could be further from the truth. Paul described our condition before Christ as outsiders. In Ephesians 2, he wrote, "Remember that formerly you who are Gentiles by birth and called 'uncircumcised' . . . were separate from Christ, excluded from citizenship in Israel and foreigners to the covenants of the promise, without hope and without God in the world" (verses 11–12). Separate, excluded, foreigners, hopeless. In the story of redemption, *we* are the strangers. *We* are the outsiders. *We* are the other.

Ever since our expulsion from Eden, the angel has barred the way back. We have wandered as strangers on the earth, seeking a place to belong. We have been wounded in our vulnerability and have ached for stability. Our sin has disconnected us from the source of life and left us in need of redemption.

From the beginning, though, God has sought to welcome us back. His perfect love has cast out fear and turned strangers into sons, the distanced into daughters. And for this reason, hospitality was a central part of the teaching of the Torah. The Israelites were called to remember their own otherness. Remembering their time in Egypt as foreigners and their wilderness wanderings as nomads was to produce compassion for the other among them.

> Do not mistreat or oppress a foreigner, for you were foreigners in Egypt. (Exodus 22:21)

> When a foreigner resides among you in your land, do not mistreat them. The foreigner residing among you must be treated as your native-born. Love them as yourself, for you were foreigners in Egypt. I am the LORD your God. (Leviticus 19:33–34)

Consideration of the strangers was even to appear in economic practices that left margin, dignity, and provision for them:

> When you reap the harvest of your land, do not reap to the very edges of your field or gather the gleanings of your harvest. Do not go over your vineyard a second time or pick up the grapes that have fallen. Leave them for the poor and the foreigner. I am the LORD your God. (Leviticus 19:9–10)

The children of Israel were to overcome fear and prejudice and show hospitality to others because this was the way their gracious God had treated them. Understanding was to lead to inclusion.

THE JESUS WAY OF HOSPITALITY

Nowhere in all recorded history do we see radical hospitality as we do in the life of Jesus. New Testament scholar Joshua Jipp noted, "The entire ministry of Jesus is appropriately captured in the phrase 'divine hospitality to the stranger and sinner.'"[8] Jesus's ministry was the rescuing love and welcome of God on display. Jesus's posture was one of inclusion and embrace. He created a portal of heaven's welcome for those who had been pushed out and shunned. Jipp also wrote, "God's hospitality is extended to his lost, broken, needy, and often stigmatized people. This divine hospitality comes to us in the person of Jesus, the divine host who extends God's hospitality to sinners, outcasts, and strangers and thereby draws them—and us—into friendship with God. God's embrace of humanity into friendship with him is the ultimate form of welcoming the stranger."[9]

If you were to trace the hospitality of Jesus through a gospel, you would find that hospitality wasn't one of Jesus's strategies; it was *the* strategy. Tim Chester, a UK pastor, outlined the theme in Luke for us:

> Luke's gospel is full of stories of Jesus eating with people:
> * In Luke 5 Jesus eats with tax collectors and sinners at the home of Levi.
> * In Luke 7 Jesus is anointed at the home of Simon the Pharisee during a meal.
> * In Luke 9 Jesus feeds the five thousand.
> * In Luke 10 Jesus eats in the home of Martha and Mary.
> * In Luke 11 Jesus condemns the Pharisees and teachers of the law at a meal.
> * In Luke 14 Jesus is at a meal when he urges people to invite the poor to their meals rather than their friends.
> * In Luke 19 Jesus invites himself to dinner with Zacchaeus.
> * In Luke 22 we have the account of the Last Supper.
> * In Luke 24 the risen Christ has a meal with the two disciples in Emmaus, and then later eats fish with the disciples in Jerusalem.
> Robert Karris concludes: "In Luke's Gospel Jesus is either going to a meal, at a meal, or coming from a meal."[10]

Jesus ate with sinners, tax collectors, and fishermen. He included and welcomed those turned into the other by the religious culture of his day. He humanized those others dismissed as outsiders and extended the welcome of God. The Pharisees used boundary markers to exclude and dehumanize. They even called the Gentiles "dogs," refusing to acknowledge their presence as people before Yahweh. But Jesus tore these boundary markers down. He replaced them with a radical welcome that still reverberates through the world today.

Unlike our culture's hospitality, which is extended to those like us and withheld from those who differ, Jesus's hospitality was scandalously unconditional. Conditional hospitality crystalizes borders. Unconditional hospitality deconstructs them. We are called to this unconditional hospitality. Philosopher Jacques Derrida commented on this, "Absolute hospitality requires that I open up my home and that I give not only to the foreigner (provided with a family name, with the social status of being a foreigner, etc.), but to the absolute, unknown, anonymous other, and that I *give place* to them, that I let them come, that I let them arrive, and take place in the place I offer them, without asking of them either reciprocity (entering into a pact) or even their names."[11] Absolute hospitality is the call of the church.

Jesus was able to model what our culture is craving—spaces of welcome where strangers, enemies, outsiders, and others can become our friends. Jesus created pockets of love in a culture of fear that formed a new kind of community in the world, something he called "the church." The church was to exist not as a haven from the world but as a place of hope for the world. To quote Jipp again, "Hospitality is the act or process whereby the identity of the stranger is transformed into that of guest. . . . The primary impulse of hospitality is to create a safe and welcoming place where a stranger can be converted into a friend. The practice of hospitality to strangers very frequently hopes to create relationships and friendships between those who were previously either alienated, at enmity, or simply unknown to one another."[12]

How do we learn to practice hospitality the way Jesus did? Let me suggest this formula:

an environment of welcome + a transformation of identity = a new humanity

If we are going to continue the life-giving, healing ministry of Jesus, we must open our hearts and lives to create environments of welcome. Jesus had the remarkable ability to draw people from the most culturally incompatible backgrounds into a new community. His disciples were nationalist zealots, cultural traitors (tax collectors), Pharisees, peasants, women, lepers, and everyone in between. He created portals of grace that gave people new identities. No longer were they defined by strict cultural categories or past sins; they were called sons and daughters of a loving Father. His environment of welcome plus the transformation of old identities, resulting in a new humanity, has changed history forever. Jesus loved and accepted people for who they really were. They could drop their masks of religiosity and performance and receive unconditional love.

People today are exhausted from having to perform and earn their way into community, so when someone welcomes them in love, hearts and humanity are restored.

I have lived in New York for fifteen years, and during this time my understanding of the city has drastically changed. During my first years in the city, Tim Keller said to me, "Many Christians move to the city because they think the city needs them, but they don't know they actually need the city."[13] I have found this to be so true. The diversity of the city—socially, politically, culturally, socioeconomically, and racially—has confronted so many stereotypes and prejudices in my heart that I didn't even know existed. Over the years my posture has changed from seeking to reach the city and change it to loving the city to serve it. I have sought to model Jesus's hospitality in order to create portals of belonging in a city that often stereotypes out of fear. With a posture of welcome, you never know when one of these portals will open and grace will break in.

CHICKEN IN A TAXI

One deficit New York has had is its lack of quality chicken fast-food restaurants. After I'd lived here for a decade, one of America's best finally opened in New York.[14]

On one occasion I was taking a taxi to our offices, which happen to be near one of these restaurants. I was preoccupied but eventually broke into a conversation with the driver. The driver began to share his story of immigration to America, the circumstances that forced him to leave his home, and the beauty of his former life. He was an incredibly well-educated man with advanced degrees, a member of the upper-middle class of his old community, but he was forced to flee because of political persecution. His credentials were not recognized in the States, and he was required to go back to graduate school to redo degrees he already had. He was working as a taxi driver as the best employment he could find, driving busy, distracted people like me around while he carried another life and vast potential inside him.

It was a powerful conversation. He went from a statistic of immigration in my head to a portrait of humanity before my eyes. I felt the humanizing of a representative group take place in my heart.

As I pulled up in front of the restaurant, I asked him whether he had ever had the food there. "No," he replied, "but I always see long lines out the front. It must be good."

"What are you doing for the next thirty minutes?" I asked him.

"Working," he said.

"If you keep the meter running, would you like to try some of the famous chicken?" I asked.

"Are you serious?" he replied.

"Yeah, mate, wait here, and I'll be back with some goodness."

So on the side of Thirty-Eighth Street, in the middle of Manhattan, two men from opposite sides of the world ate chicken and talked about their families, histories, struggles, and triumphs and their shared experience of moving to New York. For thirty minutes, in a taxi in New York, the other became a brother; a stranger, a friend.

As our time was up and I walked to our office, my heart was so full. Over chicken and lemonade, my view of immigrants was forever changed. I couldn't help but think how different New York would be if these portals of welcome became normal. If they broke out in taxis and on trains and in office buildings and in parks and everywhere in between.

And of course, it's not just New York that's in need of hospitality. Alan Hirsch, a missiologist and fellow Aussie, and Lance Ford, a missional church leader, wrote, "If every Christian family in the world simply offered good conversational hospitality around a table once a week to neighbors, we would eat our way into the kingdom of God."[15] Encounter by encounter, hospitality would deconstruct fear and reconstruct a shared humanity.

Two-Way Gift

"Above all, love each other deeply, because love covers over a multitude of sins," wrote the apostle Peter to Christians struggling to deconstruct the barriers of class, race, gender, and religion. "Offer hospitality to one another without grumbling" (1 Peter 4:8–9). The Greek word for "grumbling" means "a secret displeasure not openly avowed." It can also mean "muttering" or "a secret debate." Augustine is rumored to have had a sign on his wall that read, "He who speaks evil of an absent man or woman is not welcome at this table." The table of hospitality is a sacred space of belonging, not criticism and complaint. God is looking for a people who don't just open their homes but open their hearts. The table of hospitality isn't where we gather to criticize others or reluctantly show welcome; it's a tangible encounter with the grace of God.

In *The Divine Commodity*, Skye Jethani noted, "The English word *hospi-*

tality originates from the same Latin root as the word *hospital*. A hospital is literally a 'home for strangers.' Of course, it has come to mean a place of healing. There is a link between being welcomed and being healed." He continued, "Our homes are to be hospitals—refuges of healing radiating the light of heaven. And our dinner tables are to be operating tables—the place where broken souls are made whole again. . . . When we lower our defenses, when we remove our façades and our peepholes, and we begin to be truly present with one another—then the healing power of the gospel can begin its work."[16]

The practice of hospitality is normally understood as a privilege extended to others, but the biblical writers believed that hospitality offers a promise and gift to those who extend it. Hebrews 13:2 says, "Do not forget to show hospitality to strangers, for by so doing some people have shown hospitality to angels without knowing it." In the Scriptures, angels are messengers sent to warn or bring good news. What is perceived as a threat may actually be a promise. By refusing hospitality, we may be shutting out the help and guidance of God himself. What would have happened to Abraham if he had refused to show hospitality (Genesis 18:1–10)? What would have happened to Lot if he hadn't welcomed the strangers (Genesis 19:1–25)? What would have happened to Mary if she had refused the angel (Luke 1:26–38)? What would have happened on the road to Emmaus if the travelers hadn't welcomed Christ (Luke 24:13–32)? To use Krish Kandiah's phrasing, their biggest fear turned out to be the greatest opportunity of their lives.[17]

What will happen to us if we refuse the stranger? If we rely on cultural lenses rather than biblical ones, we may be shutting God out of our lives. Bible scholar Bob Ekblad wrote, "The Bible is locked up by theologies we absorb from our subcultures. . . . Left unchallenged, these assumptions will cause us to consciously or unconsciously look for evidence in the Bible to support our ideas."[18] Matthew 25 tells us that God has disguised himself among the broken and the poor (verses 34–40). Hospitality is the lens that lets us see through the disguise to Christ himself. Rather than robbing us of our rights, hospitality may be opening a door of eternal reward.

DINNER WITH A RACIST

Derek Black, "the heir" of American white nationalism, was not doing well at college. At 1:56 a.m. one April morning, Derek saw a post on a student message board. "Derek black: white supremacist, radio host . . . new college student???" the post read. "How do we as a community respond?"[19] Someone at the school had been doing research on terrorist groups online and stumbled on Derek's secret life. He was outed as a white supremacist. The response was visceral. Over a thousand replies were left on the message board.

Derek would recall later, "I could sit there and just read post after post on this 1,000-page message talking about how I was not welcomed there, how I didn't represent them, how they couldn't understand how I could be a part of this place they were trying to build." He called it "unsettling."[20]

Other students were unsettled as well, not knowing what to do with the racist in their midst. But then someone Derek knew from his first semester had an idea.

Matthew Stevenson was the only Orthodox Jewish student at the college. Without much of an ecosystem for Jewish thriving, he had started hosting a Friday night Shabbat dinner to foster understanding of Jewish culture and life. His regular visitors included curious Christians and atheists and people of different ethnic backgrounds. But a white nationalist who had written blatantly anti-Semitic statements? In the fall of 2011, Matthew invited Derek to join them.

Derek, after being shunned by the whole campus, decided to go. It was the only invitation he had received since news of his identity had come out. When he arrived, the group was nervous. But week after week, Derek continued to show up. Slowly, meal by meal, month by month, his views began to change. His encounter with the *other* began to shift them from the other to simply *another*. His new friends encouraged him to explore things he had previously dismissed. He took classes he previously avoided. Slowly his lens of white nationalism began to fade, and a vision of shared humanity emerged.[21] He eventually came to renounce white nationalism, even writing in the Southern Poverty Law Center's *Intelligence Report,*

> Things I have said as well as my actions have been harmful to people of color, people of Jewish descent, activists striving for opportunity and fairness for all. . . .
> I am sorry for the damage done.[22]

Around a table on a college campus, a Jew and a white supremacist encountered a portal of possibility. An environment of welcome transformed Derek's identity, and he found a new way forward.

Matthew Stevenson is a wonderful model. How about you? Whom do you know who is different enough from you that you feel uncomfortable with that person? Set the discomfort aside for now. Think about a nonthreatening invitation you can offer to get to know this person better. Then do it.

And if someone who is different from you invites you to a meal or social event, are you going to be ready to say yes, as Jesus did many times?

Spiritual writer Henri Nouwen said this decades ago (and it's more true now than ever): "Our society seems to be increasingly full of fearful, defensive, aggressive people anxiously clinging to their property and inclined to look at their surrounding world with suspicion, always expecting an enemy to suddenly appear, intrude and do harm. But still—that is our vocation: to convert . . . the enemy into a guest and to create the free and fearless space where brotherhood and sisterhood can be formed and fully experienced."[23] To create a free and fearless space—this is our vocation. Hospitality must resist fear.

Chapter 6

Honor Must Resist Contempt

Be devoted to one another in love. Honor one another above yourselves.

Romans 12:10

The way to be really despicable is to be contemptuous of other people's pain.

JAMES BALDWIN, *Giovanni's Room*

Whenever we are sure that we are among the righteous, we immediately find ourselves among the arrogant.

FLEMING RUTLEDGE, "The Bottom of the Night"

I was riding the A train from 168th Street in Manhattan down to Midtown when a mother and her young son got on. It was the middle of the morning rush, the train was packed, and there were no seats available. The child, all of seven or eight, began to wriggle and bump into people. It was clear this young boy could not adjust to his social setting. The mother, embarrassed, grabbed the child and tried to pull him in. A power dynamic quickly emerged. Eyes began to lift from their phones. In a desperate attempt to avoid further attention, the mother yanked the boy and pulled him toward her.

Now, as someone who has lived in New York for a decade and a half, I have seen almost everything that can happen on a morning commute. Nakedness, sickness, violence. Yet what came next has been memorialized in a category of its own. The child slapped his mother's hand away, looked up at her, and defiantly cursed her with the most vulgar four-letter word.

Stunned silence filled the car while the train barreled down the track. For a second the carriage held its collective breath. The weight of those words on the tongue of a child. We waited for the response, but it never came. The mother just bowed her head in shame. The boy leaned toward her in silence, and the train continued.

You could see people straining not to comment, not to correct or rebuke. In New York you never intrude or tell someone how to parent without *real* consequences. So, slowly, headphones were placed back in ears and eyes returned to their screens. But we all knew we had witnessed something deeply broken. We were getting a front-row seat to the decline of Western civilization. Seats we didn't ask for, seats we didn't want. Somewhere on the blue line, between 125th Street and Columbus Avenue, the brokenness of our culture bled in.

This culture is one of dishonor and contempt. A harsh one of both brutality and backlash. We show contempt for those who don't agree with our political views, contempt for those with different religious views, contempt for the rich, contempt for the poor, contempt for those family members who always seem to be embarrassing us and causing trouble. And we show contempt in the church. Contempt for those with different theological positions, different styles of worship, different structures of leadership, different styles of preaching. We can grow numb to the contempt in our world at large, but when children are defying their parents in such a visceral way, we are forced to face the kind of society we are becoming.

My mind has gone back to that boy many times over the years. What does the future hold for him? Where will he be in five, ten, twenty years? Whom will he marry? How will he raise his children? What will he do for a living? How will it go for him? "Children . . . 'Honor your father and mother . . . that it may go well with you'" (Ephesians 6:1–3).

How will it go? The lack of honor he showed that day on the train suggests it may not go very well.

Contempt is the feeling that someone else is beneath consideration, worthless, deserving scorn. Contempt slips so easily into our hearts these days, and it lodges there. And what's in our hearts comes out through our mouths. Christians, I'm sorry to say, are often little—if any—better than the rest of society when it comes to this failing. In fact, in addition to social and political differences, we put others down because of moral and theological arguments.

The solution is the same as in the commandment for children—show honor. Honor is the call to *recognize* the value someone possesses and *esteem* that person rightly. And when we understand that call, we can see that honor is the culture of heaven.

If we're going to show the world a better way and help ease the widespread contempt of our day, we'll have to be the leaders in showing people respect.

Honor resists contempt. But right now, it isn't doing that.

THE DEMISE OF HONOR AND THE RISE OF CONTEMPT

"What is left when honor is lost?" Publilius Syrus, a writer in the first century BC, asked of his age.[1]

Our age can provide the answer: contempt.

Many have talked about the anger in our culture, and there is evidence of that all around, but maybe we have misdiagnosed the kind of anger we are dealing with. All communities deal with conflict at various levels and disagreement about topics that range from human sexuality to urban planning. But what we are dealing with seems to be deeper than that.

In an attempt to articulate the angst, columnist Arthur Brooks described the differences between hot hate and cool hate. Hot hate, he said, is based on anger, while cool hate is based on contempt. "Cool hate can be every bit as damaging as hot hate. The social psychologist and relationship expert John Gottman was famously able to predict with up to 94 percent accuracy whether couples would divorce just by observing a brief snippet of conversation. The biggest warning signs of all were indications of contempt, such as sarcasm, sneering and hostile humor. . . . Disagreement is normal, but dismissiveness can be deadly."[2]

Contempt is causing us to dismiss entire segments of society, and it is destroying the social fabric of our lives. Contempt doesn't just cause marital divorce; it is *fracturing* long-held friendships, workplaces, and parental and sibling relationships.

America's esprit de corps used to be *E pluribus unum:* "out of many, one." At its founding, thirteen small colonies came together with the realization that they were better together, in spite of all their differences. They strained to find a way to collaborate and overcome these differences. The result was an experiment of respect and regard built on self-evident and inalienable rights. That fragile union seems to be collapsing before our eyes.

Sebastian Junger documented the grief that veterans often feel upon returning to America after serving in the military overseas. In *Tribe* he wrote, "We live in a society that is basically at war with itself."

> People speak with incredible contempt about—depending on their views—the rich, the poor, the educated, the foreign-born, the president, or the entire US government. It's a level of contempt that is usually reserved for enemies in wartime, except that now it's applied to our fellow citizens. Unlike criticism, contempt is particularly toxic because it assumes a moral superiority in the speaker. Contempt is often directed at people who have been excluded from a group or declared unworthy of its benefits. Contempt is often used by governments to provide rhetorical cover for torture or abuse. . . . People who speak with contempt for one another will probably not remain united for long.[3]

With the rise of contempt, the clock on respect and civility seems to be running out. *Ex uno plures*. "Out of one, many."

The toxic power of contempt lies in its devaluation of others. "Contempt is itself the claim to relative superiority."[4] A standard is imposed, and those who fail to meet that standard—be it moral, ethical, aesthetic, social, or related to competence—are devalued based on their failure to comply with the norm. Contempt is also toxic because it is difficult to identify in the broader range of emotions.

Psychologists have identified six basic human emotions: anger, disgust, fear, happiness, sadness, and surprise. You will notice contempt is not one of them. But Robert C. Solomon, a philosopher at the University of Texas, Austin, placed contempt on the same continuum as resentment and anger. He then nuanced it the following way:

- Resentment is anger directed toward a higher-status individual.
- Anger is directed toward an equal-status individual.
- Contempt is anger directed toward a lower-status individual.[5]

Contempt categorically devalues people and justifies its anger. This creates a dynamic of power and superiority from which most relationships never recover. Every exercise of power incorporates a faint, almost imperceptible, element of contempt for those over whom the power is exercised. One can dominate another human soul only if one despises the person one is subjugating. When contempt becomes the operating system of a society, disdain can become dangerous. All atrocities, including the Holocaust and the Rwandan genocide, started by lowering the value of others and justifying the right to dismiss and ultimately destroy them.

Bonhoeffer faced this exact challenge with the Jews of his day. The German church treated the Jews with contempt, and in devaluing and dehumanizing them, they were complicit in the deaths of over six million people made in the image of God. Though we may reassure ourselves that we would never have taken part in genocide like that, we may murder in our hearts, something Scripture decries as unacceptable in hearts designed for love (1 John 3:15).

Lowering the value of others causes us to emotionally withdraw. We are terrified about being compared to "them," as they threaten our own sense of dignity. We withdraw into small circles of sameness, places where we can elevate our worth over the worth of those we have removed ourselves from. In *Them,* Senator Ben Sasse wrote,

> Our isolation has deprived us of healthy local tribes with whom we share values and goals and ways of life that uplift us, and so we fall into "anti-tribes," defined by what we're against rather than what we're for.
>
> It's a sorry substitute for real belonging, but it's better than nothing. We might not have much in the way of community, but at least we aren't as ludicrous as those sanctimonious liberals on MSNBC, or as absurd as those blowhard conservatives on Fox. There's something comforting in joining people of a similar mind-set ("we") to denounce "them."
>
> No one wants to sit alone.
>
> And so, liberals and conservatives no longer believe the same things, we don't understand how our opponents believe what they believe, and we soothe our lonely souls with the balm of contempt.[6]

CONTEMPT AMONG THE PEOPLE OF GOD

Contempt may be the most toxic force eroding the people of God today. Contempt defined the culture of the Pharisees that distorted the covenant people of God. I have seen this same damage happen to so many in the body of Christ. Believers get drawn into contempt in the realm of politics but find they cannot isolate the attitude from other areas of their hearts. It soon bleeds into the way we see our brothers and sisters inside the Christian community.

A hermeneutic of suspicion shuts down our vulnerability, resulting in anger and fear. No church can thrive with this lurking in the pews. Because we have new-covenant hearts designed to live by grace and love, contempt in our hearts poisons us. As one novelist wrote, "Familiarity breeds contempt, for others at first, but then inwardly, contempt towards ourselves."[7] No followers of Jesus can walk in fullness and joy when they harbor cool hate in their hearts.

When contempt controls the people of God, it becomes a kind of spiritual cancer that eats away at our power and possibility. We see this attitude toward God begin to emerge in the children of Israel during their rescue from Egypt.

In the Exodus, God poured out his power and presence on the Israelites to free them from the tyranny of Pharaoh, but he could not deliver his people from the tyranny of contempt. God broke the Red Sea open, provided manna in the wilderness, forgave the golden calf incident, and led them to the border of a land flowing with milk and honey. But on the doorstep of their destiny, contempt took over and disdain destroyed their faith. Despite the good report of the two faithful spies, the giants became bigger than God, and faith turned to frustration. God incredulously asked Moses, "How long will these people treat me with contempt? How long will they refuse to believe in me, in spite of all the signs I have performed among them?" (Numbers 14:11). This disdain for God's goodness caused an entire generation to miss out on its destiny and perish in the wilderness. Instead of inheriting the promised land, those who showed contempt were not allowed in. God would not allow the cancer of contempt to be part of a culture of deliverance.

The danger of contempt is not restricted to the Old Testament. In the book of Romans, Paul wrote,

> Do you show contempt for the riches of his kindness, forbearance and patience, not realizing that God's kindness is intended to lead you to repentance?
>
> But because of your stubbornness and your unrepentant heart, you are storing up wrath against yourself for the day of God's wrath, when his righteous judgment will be revealed. (2:4–5)

Contempt diminishes the impact of God's mercy and leaves us to suffer the consequences of his wrath. Contempt cuts us off from the blessing of God.

As believers, we know that the Spirit can be grieved, and we have normally connected this grief to our sinful behavior or unbelief. But 1 Thessalonians states that the quenching is connected to contempt for the Spirit's gifts. Paul wrote, "Do not quench the Spirit. Do not treat prophecies with contempt but test them all; hold on to what is good, reject every kind of evil" (5:19–22). We grieve the Spirit when we resist his intervention in our comfortable and familiar ministries and devalue the supernatural as a necessary nuisance.

Nowhere in the Scriptures is the danger of contempt more clear than in the ministry of Jesus. This is highlighted in Mark 6:1–6, where we read:

> Jesus left there and went to his hometown, accompanied by his disciples. When the Sabbath came, he began to teach in the synagogue, and many who heard him were amazed.
>
> "Where did this man get these things?" they asked. "What's this wisdom that has been given him? What are these remarkable miracles he is performing? Isn't this the carpenter? Isn't this Mary's son and the brother of James, Joseph, Judas and Simon? Aren't his sisters here with us?" And they took offense at him.
>
> Jesus said to them, "A prophet is not without honor except in his own town, among his relatives and in his own home." He could not do any miracles there, except lay his hands on a few sick people and heal them. He was amazed at their lack of faith.

Those close to Jesus were offended by the fact that such wisdom and power could come from someone they knew. Someone so normal, someone like them. Someone with normal parents from the working class. His familiarity precluded honor. They couldn't see past the familiar to the anointing Jesus carried. They were prejudiced by proximity.

We often do the same today. We refuse to believe that those around us—

our families, our friends, and the members of our communities—could be the very ones God wants to use to shape history and bring his kingdom. We fail to see the possibility and destiny that others carry, because the familiar hinders faith.

I often wonder what could have happened in that village if they had been willing to honor Jesus. Imagine what he could have unleashed in his own town. Everyone could have been healed. All could have been set free. No one would have gone away hungry, empty, oppressed, or shamed. But without honor, all he could do was heal a few sick people. Their lack of faith amazed him. Honor gives us access to others' anointing. Contempt restricts the ability of Jesus to move. Contempt closes off; honor opens up. God goes where he is wanted.

THE KINGDOM'S OPERATING SYSTEM

Deep in our hearts, we feel sick about the hostility, dishonor, and disdain in our world. A kind of collective fatigue manifests itself in our disgust for our culture. We are exhausted by the devaluing of others but feel powerless to stop. I feel this at times after I am done looking at social media. There is so much condescension and so much anger. I feel both grieved and overwhelmed. I want to lash out, but I don't exactly know how. We don't know how to change the channel of contempt. Unity feels like a pipe dream, and healing, out of reach. Our hearts are grieved by the failure of the church as well. The way we devalue people for their theology or lack of it, different practices and traditions, and struggles with sin. Our vision of God has been lowered, his power is scarce, and his love is a rumor that's been chased away.

I believe there is a cure for the cancer of contempt: honor.

Honor is one of the most beautiful and neglected virtues in the world today. Yet talking about honor feels anachronistic. How would we hold this forth as a value in a climate like ours? Honoring others. Where or how would we even begin? Who would define what is honorable?

In other societies, honor has been the key for civility, respect, cohesion, and flourishing, and I believe by our beholding it afresh and reclaiming it in our lives, honor could produce those same things today.[8]

Christians for the most part seem to be the ones who cling to this word. Sometimes we hear about churches having honor cultures, but they rarely seem to be cultures where *everyone* is honored. The power dynamics work in such a way that the honor flows uphill to the senior leaders. Honor seems to work much as it would in the world. The most visible receive the most glory; the most gifted, the most attention. Modern media, both traditional and social, reinforce the worthiness of the charismatic and attractive. This has produced real concern that those speaking in Jesus's name are siphoning off some of the honor that he deserves.

In spite of confusion about or the abuse of honor, I've come to believe that honor is not peripheral but central to the life of the church. In the New Testament, the word for "honor" (*timáō*) means "to assign value" or "to prize."[9]

A biblical vision of honor is a life-giving source of joy to all who are touched by it.

Honor is the recognition of the value, contribution, and importance of others. "Honor is a relational or social term that identifies how people in any society evaluate one another."[10] Sometimes we can confuse glory and honor in our theology and think they are interchangeable. Making the distinction is key. Glory is inherent in something. It's the intrinsic weight something possesses. It needs no recognition (though it deserves it). Glory is not diminished by a lack of recognition. As C. S. Lewis noted, "A man can no more diminish God's glory by refusing to worship Him than a lunatic can put out the sun by scribbling the word 'darkness' on the walls of his cell."[11] Honor, however, is *recognizing* the value of something. This is where honor contains the power to transform. If contempt reduces value, honor restores it and lays a foundation for all our relationships.

Honor is the call to recognize the value in God and one another and to order our relationships around it. Honor is the operating system of the kingdom of God. How seriously have you taken the value of honor in your own life?

THE HONOR FILTER

"From now on we regard no one from a worldly point of view," wrote the apostle Paul in 2 Corinthians 5:16, meaning we no longer filter people based on cultural categories or personal preferences. We have a lens of divine value that sees every person as Christ does.

Jesus had a filter of honor for all he encountered. Regardless of the contempt their culture showed them, he saw differently. He didn't see tax collectors, prostitutes, sinners, outcasts, or Samaritans. He saw people crowned with glory, worthy of welcome and recognition in the community of God. Jesus's filter of value created a community unlike the world had ever seen. How do we reclaim this honor filter in our world today?

Honoring Others' Stories

Everyone has a backstory. We have all been shaped by pain and wounds and glories that inform how we act today. Rather than rushing to judgment, honor takes into consideration all that people have been through.

Stephen Covey shared a powerful example of how understanding someone's story honors that person's experience. One weekend while taking a train in New York, he was relishing some quiet reflection and solace. The train stopped, the doors opened, and a father and his children got on. The children began to shout and throw things and disturb the whole train. When Covey could handle it no longer, he challenged the man. "Sir, your children are really disturbing a lot of people. I wonder if you couldn't control them a little more?"

> The man lifted his gaze as if to come to a consciousness of the situation for the first time and said softly, "Oh, you're right. I guess I should do something about it. We just came from the hospital where their mother died about an hour ago. I don't know what to think, and I guess they don't know how to handle it either."
>
> Can you imagine what I felt at that moment? My paradigm shifted.

Suddenly I *saw* things differently, and because I *saw* differently, I *thought* differently, I *felt* differently, I *behaved* differently. My irritation vanished. I didn't have to worry about controlling my attitude or my behavior; my heart was filled with the man's pain. Feelings of sympathy and compassion flowed freely. "Your wife just died? Oh, I'm so sorry! Can you tell me about it? What can I do to help?" Everything changed in an instant.[12]

Knowing others' backstories releases compassion and honors the journeys that people have been on.

Honoring Others' Callings

Acts 17:26 says that God has determined the exact time and place in history in which we are to live. The Bible also says that we are "fearfully and wonderfully made" (Psalm 139:14). It goes on to say that God has prepared good works for each of us to walk in (Ephesians 2:10). We love to apply these verses to ourselves, endlessly taking personality tests to understand who we are and what our calling is. Then with great intentionality we try to honor the sacred journey God has for us. But I wonder how often we apply this same perspective to others. They, too, are here for a purpose. They, too, were made who they are for a reason. They, too, have good works to walk in. Honor doesn't just consider our own calling and doesn't just view others as those here to help us fulfill it; honor respects and supports the plans and purposes of others and considers it a deep privilege to help others realize their destiny.

Honoring Others' Sacrifices

Because we interact with people in scenes of their lives, we are often unaware of what it has cost them to reach this moment. I often encounter this lack of awareness when people are new to our church. Sometimes people come in and make extraordinary demands, heaping unrealistic expectations and hopes on our team. We do our best to love and care, but this just isn't enough for some folks. I wish I could tell them the price our team has paid to lead a church in a city like ours. But it goes both ways. Sometimes we fail to see the price people have paid to join our community, and we assume that if people don't want to serve God, they are spiritually lazy or immature. But honor seeks to understand and value the sacrifices all of us have made and to be grateful for and gentle with those with whom we relate.

Honoring Others' Gifts

We live in a world where we are drawn to the successful. In our relational economics we are quick to dismiss those whom we perceive as having low value or who can't help us in any way. But honor looks at people differently. Honor sees that everyone matters in the kingdom of God, and those most overlooked can often become the most important people in our lives. Just because someone isn't charismatic or attractive doesn't mean that person doesn't play vital roles in God's view.

When I was in my midthirties, I began to experience strong stabs of pain toward the top of my stomach. I was in an aggressive training program at the time and thought it might be muscle spasms due to the intensity of the workouts. One Sabbath, after eating a bag of Swedish Fish and barbecue chips, I began to experience strong pain. I took some aspirin and a nap, thinking it would pass. I woke up with the most extraordinary pain I had ever felt. It quickly moved beyond my threshold. My wife rushed me to the emergency room, where I paced and yelled until seen by a doctor and given drugs. It turned out I was having a gallbladder attack, and it ultimately had to be removed.

Until that moment, I had no awareness of or appreciation for the gallbladder. I took it for granted. I had never seen or heard of a gallbladder and did not recognize its role in my body. But now—oh, but now—the gallbladder means something to me. It has opened my eyes to the absolute wonder of the invisible but important parts of our bodies that go unnoticed but are vital for our health and well-being. In the same way, honor sees every person as a vital part of the body of Christ, and regardless of external cultural markers, we know every person is indispensable to God.

Paul's vision of honor startles modern ears:

> The eye cannot say to the hand, "I don't need you!" And the head cannot say to the feet, "I don't need you!" On the contrary, those parts of the body that seem to be weaker are indispensable, and the parts that we think are less honorable we treat with special honor. And the parts that are unpresentable are treated with special modesty, while our presentable parts need no special treatment. But God has put the body together, giving greater honor to the parts that lacked it, so that there should be no division in the body, but that its parts should have equal concern for each other. If one part suffers, every part suffers with it; if one part is honored, every part rejoices with it. (1 Corinthians 12:21–26)

Honor recognizes the gifts each person carries, knows they are needed in the body of Christ, and trusts the Holy Spirit, who has distributed them according to his own sovereign purpose.

Honoring Others' Futures

When I was sixteen, I dropped out of high school to work as a butcher in a meat factory in Australia. I was not the kind of person whom people met and recognized as a future leader.

When I was seventeen, I became a Christian at a Pentecostal youth camp, and my whole life changed. During that camp, the youth pastor asked for people to come to the front and share what God had done in their lives. I felt electricity in my body and knew I was meant to say something. I awkwardly went to the front and blurted out my testimony. It wasn't very clear, and I am sure it lacked theological nuance, but I had this strange sense that sharing God's truth was a part of my future.

When I finished, rather than the usual warm applause and shuffling back to my seat, the youth pastor stopped the meeting and singled me out. "Jon, when you spoke, I sensed the room listen in a different way. I believe that God may be calling you to preach his Word. Let's stop for a moment and pray over you." This prayer opened a door of destiny that I stepped through, and I have never been the same. The honor filter saw past my circumstances as a dropout into the future God had for me.

Honor sees who someone can become, not only where someone has come from. Leadership expert Dr. Joseph Umidi wrote, "Value, respect, esteem, regard, worth, and significance all flow out of the refreshing fountain of honor. Yet what leaks out from the septic tank of dishonor is disgrace, shame, humiliation, scorn, and contempt. . . . One of the most common ways we dishonor is to disregard God or people. Treating another as only part of a blurred landscape of our lives, ordinary, common, unimportant, even taken for granted, is to discount them and their unique purpose. Honor requires celebration and validation, not comfort zone toleration."[13]

I can't help but imagine the power and beauty of a community that saw everyone through an honor filter. What would happen if every person's story, calling, sacrifice, gifts, and future were held in view? If people were seen as crowned with glory and coheirs with Christ? I believe conflict would be transformed, young people would be filled with vision, the elderly would be respected, the marginalized would be empowered, and the invisible would be seen. Disagreements would be handled with respect, enemies humanized, and civility restored. This community would be unlike any other—this community would be like the kingdom of heaven on earth. Honor makes this possible in our culture of contempt.

ROAD TO RESTORATION

Honor possesses more than just the power to shape the church; it can bring healing to the world. Some sociologists have begun to recognize that many of our most troubled and broken communities are not just struggling with educational and economic deficits; they have an honor deficit. When honor has been taken from a community, the elderly are dismissed, traditions are mocked, the past is erased, hopelessness settles in, prejudice is assumed, and conflict is inevitable.

Social workers have often sought to address this brokenness through justice initiatives, government intervention, and mentoring programs, yet often these noble efforts fail to break the cycles of shame and dysfunction. I believe these approaches often fall short because they don't address the dignity that has been taken from the people.

Dr. Umidi told about a community in which another approach was tried. In essence, it was an honor intervention. The whole community was informed that a day of honor would be held, when the elderly would bring artifacts from their families' past and share their traditions and stories. The community story was told, and the strengths and gifts of the people were highlighted. An honor filter was placed over the whole community, and seeds of healing and restoration were sown.[14]

When reading about the restorative power of honor, I began to imagine a new kind of calling in the world, one that all of us can share. Not social workers but honor workers. Those who, case by case, find the pain of contempt in a person's life and restore a sense of honor. As the people of God, we would disrupt the damage done by the callousness of contempt and usher in the culture of honor. Philip Yancey noted,

> Jesus was the first world leader to inaugurate a kingdom with a heroic role for losers. He spoke to an audience raised on stories of wealthy patriarchs, strong kings, and victorious heroes. Much to their surprise, he honored instead people who have little value in the visible world: the poor and meek, the persecuted and those who mourn, social rejects, the hungry and thirsty. His stories consistently featured "the wrong people" as heroes: the prodigal, not the responsible son; the good Samaritan,

not the good Jew; Lazarus, not the rich man; the tax collector, not the Pharisee. As Charles Spurgeon . . . expressed it, "His glory was that He laid aside His glory, and the glory of the church is when she lays aside her respectability and her dignity, and counts it to be her glory to gather together the outcasts."[15]

What a glory to gather the outcasts! What a joy to lay aside our respectability for the sake of others. The world is aching for a community of honor. May it begin with us. Honor must resist contempt.

Chapter 7

Love Must Resist Hate

Love is stronger than fear, life stronger than death, hope
stronger than despair. We have to trust that the risk of loving
is always worth taking.

HENRI NOUWEN, *Bread for the Journey*

Forgiveness is the only way to reverse the irreversible flow
of history.

Attributed to HANNAH ARENDT

Father, forgive them, for they do not know what they are doing.

Luke 23:34

In 2001, in a Belgian courtroom, four defendants from the central African nation of Rwanda stood trial. Two of them were Benedictine nuns, both wearing their habits. These women looked like saints out of place, humbled, heads bowed, hesitancy in their stance. Sister Maria Kisito (thirty-six) and Sister Gertrude (forty-two), the mother superior who oversaw a convent in Rwanda, were on trial for facilitating murder.

In April 1994, the country exploded in the terror of genocide. The Hutu dominant power ordered soldiers and militiamen to exterminate the minority Tutsi community. Thousands of Tutsis fleeing for their lives sought sanctuary in the convent. To their horror, Sister Gertrude asked the Hutu militia to re-move the Tutsis from the convent. The militiamen started shooting and slash-ing the refugees, until more than seven thousand Tutsis were killed.

At the trial, Sister Gertrude protested her innocence, but survivors testified that she was definitely an accomplice. They reported, for example, that the two nuns had handed gasoline to the militiamen so they could set fire to the con-vent garage, where around five or six hundred of the Tutsis had fled. Sister Kisito even reportedly provided dried leaves that helped fan the flames. Those seeking to escape the burning garage were hacked to death.

The nuns—both Hutus—escaped to Belgium. And that is why they were among the group in a courtroom in Brussels, facing a jury for their crimes.

On June 8, 2001, after a seven-week trial, both sisters were found guilty and sentenced to twelve- and fifteen-year terms. How could they have done it, two women who had vowed to serve Jesus? A *New York Times* article closes its account of the trial with these words: "Justice is built to establish the facts of evil. It cannot explain them."[1]

Explaining hate. How can we do that?

Yet hatred is far from being a rare quality or something that only shows up in shocking cases like that of the two nuns abetting genocide in Rwanda. It's a tendency that's endemic to the sinful human heart. It is destructive to both hater and hated. It's a contradiction of the will of God. If we give in to it, as it is so easy to do and as so many others around us are doing, we'll lose the ability to witness to a Lord who said, "Father, forgive them, for they do not know what they are doing" (Luke 23:34). Love must resist hate.

TWO MINUTES HATE

I remember the first time I read George Orwell's book *1984*. It seemed so dystopian. So far from reality. So far from the world I was living in. Despite the lack of resonance, though, there was one scene that was so visceral it has stuck with me over the years. That scene was the Two Minutes Hate.

In the novel, the citizens of Oceania are required to watch propaganda about their enemy and for two minutes every day scream pure hate. This is the famous scene where everyone is looking at a giant screen, all yelling and cursing at the top of their lungs. Orwell wrote,

The horrible thing about the Two Minutes Hate was not that one was obliged to act a part, but that it was impossible to avoid joining in. Within thirty seconds any pretense was always unnecessary. A hideous ecstasy of fear and vindictiveness, a desire to kill, to torture, to smash faces in with a sledge-hammer, seemed to flow through the whole group of people like an electric current, turning one even against one's will into a grimacing, screaming lunatic. And yet the rage that one felt was an abstract, undirected emotion which could be switched from one object to another like the flame of a blowlamp.[2]

During the Two Minutes Hate, people get so carried away by their emotions that they are known to physically manifest hate by lashing out at the air or throwing things at the screen, as Julia does in the novel.

In the book, the purpose of the Two Minutes Hate is to release the angst and the frustration the citizens feel about having to live such controlled and manipulated lives. When the hate and rage are misdirected toward a supposed enemy, the powers that be are able to distract and enslave the people for their own sinister purposes.

Orwell didn't invent Two Minutes Hate; similar propaganda was used in various wars around the world to generate anger and hate for the enemy. But Orwell showed the way that technology could collectively manufacture hate among us.[3]

Given the role of the media today, the polarization of our politics, and the presence of a twenty-four-hour income-producing news cycle, we are slowly being trained to participate in our own Two Minutes Hate. We are told who is deplorable and who is worthy of respect. We are told who our enemies are and why they present a savage threat to us. Looking at a TV, computer, or phone screen is a micro version of the Two Minutes Hate. Things are not presented to us in a fair, nuanced, or civil way. Hate is being cultivated one social media post at a time. Each fifteen-second sound bite or meme is training us to release our hate on our enemies. The trickle effect over time poisons our hearts, allowing contempt and bitterness to seep in and training us to misidentify our enemies.

We have all been concerned about the use of social media by outside forces to manipulate the American political process. But to be honest, as a pastor, I am far more concerned about the manipulation of our hearts on a daily basis through cultural forces. You cannot show compassion to those you are being trained to despise. Yet over and over I see signs that some parts of the Christian church are no different from our culture—and really no different from the rage-filled Oceanians—in unleashing hate on people God made in his image. The way we talk about politicians we disagree with, the way we talk about sexual minorities, the way we talk about other nations all indicate that our hearts have been poisoned by our culture. We live in a time that seems more hateful than ever. Here, clearly, is a part of the culture that faith must resist. But it's not just cultural. It's personal.

HATRED COMES HOME

On top of the media manufacturing hate, they are also manipulating language so that it's almost unrecognizable. Today the word *hate* describes any kind of disagreement with a person, his or her worldview, ideas, or ideology. The term *hate* once carried a deeper meaning, a word used with restraint in only the strongest cases. But today, if you don't approve of a person's choices and simply express an alternative opinion, you are accused of hate. "Why do you have to be so hateful?" is a cliché.

Nevertheless, hatred truly is a universal failing. If someone loudly represents a social, political, or religious viewpoint we strongly disagree with—we hate. If someone hurts or betrays us—we hate. If we feel threatened—we hate. If we are treated unjustly—we hate. If someone rejects our love—our love can ominously invert and we hate.

The horrendous attack by the white supremacist Dylann Roof at Emanuel African Methodist Episcopal Church in Charleston, South Carolina, shows us what hate looks like. In June 2015, the twenty-one-year-old Roof sat in on an evening prayer meeting, then opened fire with a handgun, killing nine people and wounding another. All the victims were African Americans. Roof stated later that he hoped to inspire a race war.

Did he later come to his senses and think, *What have I done?* Did remorse set in?

In his jail cell, he wrote, "I would like to make it crystal clear I do not regret what I did. I am not sorry. I have not shed a tear for the innocent people I killed. . . . I have shed a tear of self-pity for myself. I feel pity that I had to do what I did in the first place."[4] That is what hate—implacable hate—looks like.

Our hatred may not seem as severe as this. But it's on the same continuum. It's the same thing. The Bible equates hate with murder (1 John 3:15).

Hate is so sadly everyday. I'm often surprised at the level of anger that lodges in a soul from bullying during school years. Sometimes we hate our parents, who sought to control us and dictate our future. Sometimes we hate former lovers who broke our hearts and abused our trust. Sometimes we hate entire ethnic groups based on a bad experience with an individual. Other times it's coworkers who stole the credit or diminished our contribution.

Whom have you hated over the course of your lifetime? Whom might you still hate today? You might be able to hide your hatred from others, but you can't become an instrument God uses for good unless you first admit your problem with hatred to yourself and to God.

You have your own struggles with hate, and I have mine. The question for both of us is, What are we going to do about it? Jesus has the answer.

ENEMY LOVE

Hate isn't the only word we misuse on a daily basis. We abuse the word *love* in much the same way.

Love has become a surface-level word conveying almost nothing. "I love Fridays." "I love cookies." "I love my wife." "I love that show." "I love God." Our culture has a wide range of instances where the word *love* is acceptable. We "love" almost everything that we feel positive about, just as we "hate" everything that carries even an ounce of negativity. We have taken a rich, nuanced word and flattened it beyond recognition. But there is a deeper meaning to the word *love,* a truer meaning.

Agapē is a term that Christians used to redefine love. It carries the idea of others-centered, sacrificial care. It is deep love, costly love. It is the love that God showed for us in Christ. Sacrificial, others-centered, covering love.

Jesus had a unique perspective on how we should engage our enemies, those we naturally hate:

> Love your enemies, do good to those who hate you, bless those who
> curse you, pray for those who mistreat you. If someone slaps you on
> one cheek, turn to them the other also. If someone takes your coat,
> do not withhold your shirt from them. Give to everyone who asks
> you, and if anyone takes what belongs to you, do not demand it back.
> Do to others as you would have them do to you.
>
> If you love those who love you, what credit is that to you? Even
> sinners love those who love them. And if you do good to those who
> are good to you, what credit is that to you? Even sinners do that. And
> if you lend to those from whom you expect repayment, what credit is
> that to you? Even sinners lend to sinners, expecting to be repaid in full.
> But love your enemies, do good to them, and lend to them without
> expecting to get anything back. Then your reward will be great, and
> you will be children of the Most High, because he is kind to the

ungrateful and wicked. Be merciful, just as your Father is merciful.
(Luke 6:27–36)

To understand the full implications of this radical teaching, you have to
understand the context in which Jesus ministered.

In their recent history, the Jewish community had tasted moments of freedom as a result of the Maccabean rebellion and the Hasmonean dynasty. After
almost five hundred years of oppression, through courage and the help of God,
they were able to throw off the yoke of their oppressors and defeat Antiochus,
a brutal leader who had demanded pagan worship, outlawed circumcision, and
desecrated the temple of God. Mattathias and then his son Judas the Hammer
rose up and reestablished the law and priesthood and were able to give their
land self-rule in accordance with their traditions.

But then came the Romans. These ultimate imperialists conquered the
Jewish homeland and absorbed them into their territory, again throwing the
yoke of pagan leadership over the Jews' shoulders. The Jews' hatred of oppression, coming after a respite of freedom, must have been intense. Who would
deliver them this time?

The Jews knew that the Old Testament prophecies announced that the
Messiah would sit on the throne of King David, and David had been a skilled
military leader. He routed their enemies and established Jerusalem as a place
of power. So during the Roman occupation, perhaps more than ever, the Jews
longed for the Davidic Messiah to come at last. A group known as the
Zealots—political terrorists who resisted and sabotaged the Romans—in particular looked for the imminent arrival of a military deliverer.

Into this landscape of heaving emotions and eager expectations came Jesus.

When Jesus began preaching, something stirred in the hearts of the people. He spoke about God's kingdom; he spoke about God breaking in and his
rule being established on earth. Jesus was a miracle worker who could raise the
dead and cast out demons. If he could do that to evil spirits, imagine what he
could do to the Romans!

Yet, as the people followed him, his teaching bewildered them. He wouldn't give a clear answer to their questions about taxation and Caesar. He seemed to indicate that God's love was for all, not just the Jews. And imagine their collective shock when he commanded, "Love your enemies, do good to those who hate you" (Luke 6:27). People must have been dumbfounded. Jesus was building a movement and amassing followers, but instead of calling them to violent revolution, he was calling them to enemy love. He called them to pray for those ruling over them and go above and beyond in obeying orders (Matthew 5:41, 44).

In doing so, Jesus was redefining a rabbinical teaching popular in his time. Leviticus 19:18 says, "Do not seek revenge or bear a grudge against anyone among your people, but love your neighbor as yourself. I am the LORD." This was interpreted by many rabbis to mean, "Love your *Jewish* neighbors." Love those who are like you. But Jesus did the impossible and recategorized enemies as neighbors, enlarged the tent of welcome so that all could fit, and scandalized the leaders of his day by talking about a kingdom that was established not by military conquest but by overcoming hatred with love. They were not to destroy their enemies but to convert them into members of the beloved community through sacrificial care.

Jesus's call to love, in contrast to the teaching of his day, was broad and deep and included even enemies. He was teaching a transformative kind of living, a countercultural vision of a kingdom whose citizens embodied a new way. The Sermon on the Mount was a definitive charter for a new-covenant community through which Jesus sought to sculpt a people who could show the world an entirely different vision of God.

There's a reason we are called to love this way—it is that Jesus first loved us this way (1 John 4:19). This is the heart of the Christian gospel. We must thank God for enemy love, because we were the enemies of God. Colossians 1:21–22 says, "Once you were alienated from God and were enemies in your minds because of your evil behavior. But now he has reconciled you by Christ's physical body through death to present you holy in his sight, without blemish and free from accusation." God loved us even when we were his enemies. Jesus died for us while we were enemies of God. Jesus's kingdom is the kind of kingdom where enemies are invited, loved, forgiven, justified, sanctified, and made sons and daughters of God. They then join God in his mission of extending that radical love of enemies to the world.

THE JOHN 3:16 OF THE EARLY CHURCH

Preston Sprinkle is the author of the provocative book *Fight*. He wrote in a blog post,

> Jesus's command to "love your enemies" was the most popular verse in the early church. It was quoted in 26 places by 10 different writers in the first 300 years of Christianity, which makes it *the* most celebrated command among the first Christians. Matthew 5:44 was the so-called John 3:16 of the early church. And enemy-love was the hallmark of the Christian faith. Other religions taught that people should love their neighbors. They even taught forgiveness for those who wronged them. But actually *loving your enemy*? Only Jesus and his followers took love this far. Because this is how far the love of God extends to us—"while we were God's *enemies*" Christ loved us.
>
> Christians no longer distinguish between neighbors and enemies. Through the death of Jesus, we are swept up into God's love for all people—even enemies like us. The one who loves his enemies can no longer have any enemies. He is left only with neighbors.[5]

When the early Christians were being martyred, they forgave those who took their lives. Rather than defending themselves or seeking to save their own lives, they simply turned the other cheek and died with joy. They loved the Roman Empire to its knees.

Not that there's anything wrong with promoting John 3:16, but what if we were to make Matthew 5:44 just as prominent in our own minds, enshrining it as a daily operating principle? What if, when the office atheist goes into his faith-mockery routine, we showed him how we cared about him? What if, when our in-law who is on the other side of the political fence starts a tirade demeaning our party, we responded respectfully and kindly? What if, when a bully starts picking on us, we reacted out of love rather than fear or anger?

The gladiatorial arena is back. It can be transformed again.

But only if we're ready to act on our faith.

LOVE-FORWARD LIVING

Many of us today know the power of enemy love. We are ashamed when believers treat enemies in the way of the world and are moved when believers show enemies love. We're disappointed in ourselves when we take a backward step and slip into habits of hatred that we thought we had rid ourselves of. So, how can we develop a habit of dealing with our enemies in a Christlike way?

Few people in the history of American Christianity illustrated this approach to love better than Dr. Martin Luther King Jr. He was the target of almost-unprecedented hate from his political and cultural enemies. His belief in Jesus's teachings and enemy love was regularly tested and its power shown.

Once, while he was giving a speech in Birmingham, Alabama, a two-hundred-pound white man rushed the stage and began pummeling King. The man was so filled with hate that he wanted to physically crush his enemy. As King's aides rushed to his defense, King responded as Jesus did. He didn't retreat to a room to pray. He didn't bless the man from a distance. He didn't press charges and then visit him in prison. He immediately moved in to protect his enemy, engulfing the man in a bear hug. He became his assailant's protector. He held him, shielding him from harm, and soon the crowd began to sing the movement songs of justice and peace.

Later, King introduced the man to the crowd as if he were a valued invited guest. The man's name was Roy James, a twenty-four-year-old New Yorker and member of the American Nazi Party. As a response to this proactive enemy love, James broke down and wept in King's embrace.[6] King's proactive enemy love disrupted the power of hate in a prophetic and powerful way.

WHAT STARTED AS ROAD RAGE

Though we may not have a call to such dramatic acts of enemy love, every day we will have smaller moments that give us the opportunity to be proactive in love and create space for reconciliation. We will have our own personal and cultural chances to turn the other cheek, go the extra mile, give our garments away (Matthew 5:39–41).

I was reminded of the way these opportunities show up when a friend told me a story.

The day before, he had been driving down a street in a predominantly Jewish neighborhood of New York when he saw a car hastily reversing out of a driveway just in front of him. "Instead of letting the person back up," my friend said, "I honked my horn several times and sped through like the jerk that I am." An accident was avoided at that point.

But moments later, my friend pulled up at a stoplight and, in his mirror, saw the car he had passed. The driver of the other car passed my friend on the left during the red light and then tried to make a right turn from the left-hand lane. His car smashed into my friend's car.

Both men got out of their cars, and things got a little heated. The other driver was a young man and was obviously Jewish because he was wearing a prayer shawl. There was a synagogue right there, and several other Jewish men came out and joined in the argument. "It was kind of a big scene," remembered my friend. "I felt it was quickly becoming me against the Jewish community." An incident of road rage was turning into something resembling a riot.

Thankfully, just then a man—also Jewish—came up and said he had been a witness to the accident. He declared flatly that it was the other driver's fault. Emotions began to cool at that point.

The cop who showed up on the scene and interviewed both drivers wrote a ticket for the driver who crashed into my friend's car. My friend shook the cop's hand and walked to his car, intending to drive away. Instead, though, he sat there in the driver's seat for a while.

"I asked myself a dangerous question," my friend said. "Who else is going to show Jesus in this situation if not me?"

So my friend got out of his banged-up car and walked over to the other driver. "To be completely honest and fair," my friend said to the man, "even though the accident is your fault, we're actually both at fault because we were both driving offensively and we let our emotions get the better of us. We should be quick to listen, slow to speak, and slow to become angry, because anger doesn't produce the righteousness God desires" (see James 1:19–20).

They confessed their sins of anger to each other and to God right there on the sidewalk. "It was a strange, crazy moment," my friend recalled.

The two men decided to visit some auto shops together, getting estimates on the cost of fixing their cars. In the end another friend from our community paid for all the repairs out of pocket so the at-fault driver's insurance wouldn't be touched.

Then they had lunch at a kosher restaurant, where they shared their life stories. The other man lived in the projects and had had a difficult life. He used to be homeless and down and out in Amsterdam, until a Christian man gave him shelter and a job. Though he is deep in Judaism, in many strange ways he's had encounters with Christians. The incident with my friend was just the latest. The man said it was all shining a light on his Jewish faith.

My friend summed it up: "We've become friends, going from wanting to punch each other in the face to shaking hands and laughing and agreeing to become more peaceful drivers. So in all, I have no idea how God works, but I do know *that* he works. The devil tries to use anger to destroy us, but if we let God into our moments of anger and do his thing, man, he flips the script so awesomely."

Driving around town. Hearing each other's stories. Showing grace. In small moments that become life-changing moments, love resists hate.

CROSSING ENEMY LINES

In September 1219, Saint Francis decided to take enemy love seriously. Famous as the wealthy young merchant who sold his possessions to follow Jesus, he longed to visit the Muslim world and preach to Muslims. He made three attempts to go, but his first two tries came up short. He finally made it in 1219, during the Fifth Crusade, this one taking place in Egypt.

The Muslim force of eighty thousand was being commanded by an Egyptian sultan, al-Kamil, and the Christian crusaders, only forty thousand strong, were led by a Catholic cardinal, Pelagio Galvani. Another leader of the Crusaders urged Pelagio to negotiate peace with the sultan. But Pelagio refused, insisting it was time for a major offensive, even with such a meager force. On the day of the battle, Francis pleaded with the soldiers to stop where they were, certain it was not God's will for them to fight. Despite his entreaties, the Christians surged forward. Thousands of them were killed. Unexpectedly, the sultan put forward another peace treaty, and again the cardinal refused, hoping to conquer all of Egypt. Francis was so grieved by this situation that he decided to maneuver past the front lines in an effort to see the sultan. He had no official papers. No official endorsement. It was likely he would be killed on the spot, assumed to be a soldier or a spy. He wandered across the bloody battlefield all the way to the enemy camp, where he was captured. He said he wanted to speak to al-Kamil. Instead of killing him, the Muslim soldiers took him to the sultan. The sultan asked Francis whether he was ready to convert to Islam. Francis told him he was there to see whether the sultan would like to meet Jesus. The sultan replied by saying he couldn't have a conversation about religion without his religious scholars, so he called them all in, and they spoke for a long time about Christianity and Islam. The sultan was so moved by Francis's boldness, his conviction, his love, and his humility that he offered him riches for his bravery. Francis, who had renounced wealth, declined the sultan's offer and was released to the other side. Though the crusade ultimately continued, Francis played a prophetic role of enemy love in a sea of enemy hate. His love was proactive, risky, and a symbol of hope during one of the greatest stains in Christian history.[7] His small act of defiance created a new vision of what love can look like in a culture of crusading hate.

And Francis was just following his master, Jesus. Christ himself was the one who crossed every barrier of sin that we had set up against him. Christ came to bring us the peace of the gospel when we waged a war of sin, not just risking himself but giving himself in sacrificial love to bring us to God. What would it look like if followers of Jesus crossed borders of hate in the middle of our current cultural crusades to show Jesus's love in a tangible way to our enemies? Would you be willing to cross those lines and offer love to your enemies? What would change in our violent world if Christians crossed those lines in courtrooms and prisons and workplaces and communities and homes?

THE DOOR TO ENEMY LOVE

In one such courtroom, the trial of Dylann Roof began. To listen to the heart-ache and cries of the victims' families is almost too much to bear. It is a necessary reminder that enemy love is costly. It's supernatural. It's a sign of God in our midst.

Our enemies hurt us. Our enemies abuse us. Our enemies do violence to us. This can cause horrific trauma and require deep healing, boundaries, and grief. Jesus, however, experienced all this suffering and still insisted on love. He extended costly forgiveness to those who crucified him.

The statements from the victims' families at the trial show this sort of costly grace. These were statements spoken through pain but also statements of biblical resolve.

Nadine Collier, the daughter of murdered victim Ethel Lance, said to

Roof, "You took something very precious from me. I will never talk to her again. I will never, ever hold her again. But I forgive you. And have mercy on your soul."

The sister of another victim, DePayne Middleton-Doctor, said, "One thing that DePayne always enjoined in our family . . . is she taught me that we are the family that love built. We have no room for hating, so we have to forgive."

If you are struggling with hate, it very likely is because you have suffered real hurt. Let the hating stop here, now. Forgive your enemy. This will open the door so that you may begin to love as Christ loves.

Alana Simmons, another relative to make a statement at the Dylann Roof trial, said that the pleas for Roof's soul proved that "hate won't win."[8]

Hate won't win. That is the cry from the cross. *Hate won't win.* That is the cry from the courtroom. *Hate won't win.* That is the cry God asked from those who bear his name. *Hate won't win.* For love always has—and love always will—resist the tyranny of hate.

Chapter 8

Sacrifice Must Resist Privilege

Do nothing out of selfish ambition or vain conceit. Rather, in humility value others above yourselves, not looking to your own interests but each of you to the interests of the others.

Philippians 2:3–4

Tradition has it that whenever a group of people has tasted the lovely fruits of wealth, security and prestige it begins to find it more comfortable to believe in the obvious lie and to accept it as normal that it alone is entitled to privilege.

STEVE BIKO, "Black Consciousness and the Quest for a True Humanity"

It's 3:45 a.m., and I am standing in line at an Immigration and Naturalization Service center on the outskirts of Dallas. I am surrounded by people who speak Spanish and am struggling to make sense of where to go and what to do. It's 1999, and after marrying an American, I am in the process of changing my visa status from student to resident. I am in a new legal category. I am an immigrant. It's so early that my eyes are burning, but to my shock, I am nowhere near the front of the line. If you don't get here well before the crack of dawn, this can be an all-day affair. It appears people have been standing for hours. I try to ask those in front of me what to do, but no one within range seems to speak English. I resign myself to being herded through the process as human cattle. I pull out a book and begin to read.

After some time, I sense a small commotion. A man in formal clothing is walking down the line, asking questions. I see a slight stir of activity and wait till he comes to me. He pauses in front of me. "Do you speak English?" he asks.

"Yes," I reply. "I'm from Australia."

Something shifts in his countenance. "What visa process are you working on?"

I talk with him for a few minutes, and his whole demeanor seems to change. "Follow me," he says. To my surprise, he walks me from my place near the back of the line to the front of the line. I walk past the people who set their alarms for earlier than I did. Past the people whose skin is darker than mine. Past the people who believe that immigration should be respectful and based on the legal system and not the social one. Past the people who seem resigned to this sort of thing happening. I want to protest. I want to lift a shout of praise. I am embarrassed. I am ecstatic. I feel profoundly grateful for the hours I will save and the chance to get back to my new American life. But I feel something else as well. Something hard to describe. A kind of unease about what has happened stains the whole experience.

I am fairly new to the US immigration system, and so far my experience has been relatively painless. I've filled out papers; I've met with a lawyer. But for other people in line, those whose reply was *"Lo siento. No hablo Inglés,"* this experience may be one of the most painful of their lives. As I stand there, the resigned gaze of those behind me glazing over, the word for the experience slowly forms in my mind. *Privilege.* For the first time in my life, I have recognized the tangible fruit of privilege.

Culturally, we're encouraged to take advantage of our privilege. To protect it. To enjoy it. What else would you want to do with it?

But that is not the way of Jesus. As the Son of God, he had more privilege than any of us will ever know. As the Son of Man born in a stable and laid in a manger, as the Messiah with no place to lay his head, and finally as the Lamb of God hanging on the cross, he gave up privilege to a more profound extent than anyone else could ever match. Yet in all this, he modeled for us what to do with our blessings and opportunities: use them for others.

Sacrifice must resist the selfish enjoyment of privilege.

PRIVILEGE: WHAT IS IT?

Privilege is one of the most controversial words in our world today. It can trigger both outrage and scorn. Privilege and the controversy surrounding it has brought a deep philosophical divide between rights and responsibility. We need to understand privilege if we are going to see how we might be implicated in it.

One social justice organization defined *privilege* this way: *privilege* is "unearned access to resources (social power) that are only readily available to some people because of their social group membership; an advantage, or immunity granted to or enjoyed by one societal group above and beyond the common advantage of all other groups."[1]

According to South African writer Sian Ferguson, privilege can be accumulated in myriad ways—through race, religion, class, gender, sexual orientation, and even citizenship. Possessing privilege in one of these areas will readily provide cultural power and opportunities.[2]

To highlight this in visual form, Daysha Edewi created a video for BuzzFeed entitled "What Is Privilege?" She gathered a group of people and had them stand on a line. All participants started on the line, showing their equality in worth. They were then asked a series of questions based on their life experience. Each question moved the respondents either forward or backward, visualizing the effects of privilege in a cultural setting. The questions included these:

- If your parents worked nights or weekends, take one step back.
- If you do not normally fear sexual assault, take one step forward.
- If English was not the primary language of your household, take one step back.
- If you came from a supportive family environment, take one step forward.
- If you've tried to change your speech or mannerisms to gain credibility, take one step back.
- If your mistakes are not attributed to your racial or gender group, take one step forward.[3]

In this framework, privilege is understood primarily as a structural and systemic issue that contributes to the inequality we see in our world today.

As an immigrant whose tenure in this nation has been short, I discussed this issue with an African American friend who has multigenerational roots in this country. He gave me an intriguing analogy to articulate how this process has unfolded over time. "Imagine there's a group of people playing Monopoly. They play for one hour. By this time, all the best properties are taken and loaded up with hotels. Then you're invited to join the game. But, starting off, you have no money. So you try to get around to 'pass go.' However, instead of it being a game of joy, it quickly becomes a game of fear. You pray and hope for luck to not land on a property already owned by another player, one who established their assets before you were even allowed to play. After playing a few rounds, you basically lose all that you have been able to scrape together and eventually realize the safest place in the game is jail."

This analogy stayed with me for days, and as I walked slowly through the city and thought about my journey and those of our faith community, it was as if I had been given a new set of eyes. Things I took for granted, things handed to me—the resources that surrounded me came with such ease. They were available if I simply reached out.

Not everyone has the same access.

UNDERSTANDING THE COMPLEXITY
OF UNDERPRIVILEGE

The term *intersectionality* stems from legal scholar Kimberlé Crenshaw, who coined it in a 1989 essay entitled "Demarginalizing the Intersection of Race and Sex."

> Consider an analogy to traffic in an intersection, coming and going in all four directions. Discrimination, like traffic through an intersection, may flow in one direction, and it may flow in another. If an accident happens in an intersection, it can be caused by cars traveling from any number of directions and, sometimes, from all of them. Similarly, if a Black woman is harmed because she is in the intersection, her injury could result from sex discrimination or race discrimination. . . .
> But it is not always easy to reconstruct an accident.[4]

Intersectionality means there are all sorts of interacting pieces, which makes it hard to decipher the exact source of the injustice. If you are born with limited privilege, trying to cross a busy street is difficult. There are forces everywhere—economic, racial, religious, family, and educational. So many things could be hindering your journey. Yet you can't quite determine what they are.

In this cultural framework, underprivilege is something that hinders flourishing. To be clear, it's not that opportunity and advancement are unavailable; it's just that a privileged perspective fails to take into account the effort and energy required to overcome those barriers to entry. There is a complex web of forces that work together to raise or restrain different groups of people.

A pastoral situation with one of our parishioners highlighted this for me. A man I will call Jarod continually dealt with a frustrating and paralyzing web of issues that from my perspective were easy to solve. It wasn't until I suspended my judgment and entered his world that I saw a different reality.

Jarod always needed help financially from the church. Never large amounts, but a series of asks resulted in a conversation about financial responsibility. Our team just couldn't understand how he couldn't scrape some savings together and move on in his life. But a deeper reality emerged, a web of economic disadvantages and barriers that most of us never have to face.

Jarod grew up in an underresourced community. There were few legal ways to make any real money as a young man, and he ended up going to prison. Upon release, it was hard to find meaningful work, hard to get a proper bank account, hard to live barely above minimum wage. This led to a cycle of borrowing from predatory lenders and struggling to pay back the loans. Phone contracts were hard to get because of his credit score and history, meaning he had to pay cash, month to month, in person. This required him to drive, which resulted in a parking ticket. The ticket was almost half a paycheck—an amount he couldn't afford—which resulted in his car being towed. Without his car, it was incredibly hard to get to work. His phone was cut off because he couldn't drive to pay the bill. He got caught in delays with public transportation one day on the way to work, but without a phone, he couldn't call to say he would be late. He lost his job. He couldn't get the money together to pay the parking ticket, towing fees, and pound fees, and the city was threatening to auction his car. He came to the church for help. He came angry. He came disheartened.

When we heard his story, this web of challenge became so clear. The smallest thing turned into a net of obstacles that individually were bearable but, knotted together, seemed so hard to deal with. The energy required to get back to zero—let alone get ahead—created a cycle of disillusionment and frustration. Maybe it would be better to do a little dealing on the side, just for a few months. He asked whether the church could help break the cycle.[5]

I have never given a conscious thought to these things in my adult life. I get a phone contract or a bank account, and I avoid tickets and make calls, with little trouble. But these things have been handed to me. They come with my class and social setting. Navigating moments like these is effortless for me. But for many others, what we take for granted has to be fought for, and battle fatigue is its own form of oppression. If we want to become more like Christ, we've got to understand not only our own privilege but also how others struggle in a lack of privilege.

To be clear, I am not trying to preach a gospel of critical theory, nor do I commend it as a worldview for followers of Jesus.[6] But there are truths about the systemic nature of injustice, the history of our society, and Jesus's concern for the marginalized that are key implications of the gospel and our discipleship. In our fear of worldly ideologies, we can miss kingdom opportunities. The gospel has not just personal implications but cultural and social ones that manifest themselves in tangible and structural ways when put into practice.

REDIRECTING PRIVILEGE

There are two common reactions among those who are considered privileged: defensiveness about our rights and an appeal to personal responsibility.

- *Defensiveness.* It is not uncommon to hear statements such as these: "I've worked for everything I have. I haven't taken advantage of anybody else. I've taken responsibility for my own life. I'm not relying on the government or other people. Everything I have I've earned. Nothing has been given to me." Or they say, "Look. I've only got a limited amount of margin. Not my people, not my problem."
- *Responsibility.* From this perspective, getting ahead in America is easy. "Finish high school, don't get pregnant out of wedlock, and get a job. If you do these things, you will not be poor in America. However, if you fail to do these things, you will likely be poor regardless of the color of your skin." What they're saying is something like this: "Accept responsibility for your life. Just do the right thing, and life will go well for you. The past doesn't affect the present this much. Move on; make something of yourself."

Is this how Jesus would react?

Though these cultural responses perhaps contain elements of truth,[7] are they the dominant lens through which we should look at injustice or disparity? Is this the attitude we see in the life of Jesus? In Luke 22, Jesus spoke to this in a startling way. The context is fascinating. Jesus had washed the disciples' feet and was celebrating the Passover. He was about to give his life away and empty himself of his rights so that others could thrive. We read,

> A dispute also arose among them as to which of them was considered
> to be greatest. Jesus said to them, "The kings of the Gentiles lord it
> over them; and those who exercise authority over them call them-
> selves Benefactors. But you are not to be like that. Instead, the greatest
> among you should be like the youngest, and the one who rules like
> the one who serves. For who is greater, the one who is at the table or
> the one who serves? Is it not the one who is at the table? But I am
> among you as one who serves. You are those who have stood by me in
> my trials. And I confer on you a kingdom, just as my Father conferred
> one on me, so that you may eat and drink at my table in my kingdom
> and sit on thrones, judging the twelve tribes of Israel." (verses 24–30)

This scene in Jesus's life is almost laughable. Jesus had told his disciples that one of them would betray him and that he would have his body broken and blood poured out as a costly sacrifice of love, and he had washed their feet as a servant (verses 19–21; John 13:4–10). Then in the middle of all this, a dispute broke out among them as to which one of them could be considered the greatest. Jesus was about to die a horrific death, and all they could do was focus on maintaining and advancing personal status. I sometimes wonder whether this is how we look to the world around us. There are brokenness and need everywhere, Jesus has clearly called us to give ourselves away for the sake of others, and instead, we are fighting about how to advance our individual lives and happiness.

Yet Jesus laid a foundation from which we can steward our privilege for the sake of others without any fear. He told them, "I confer on you a kingdom, just as my Father conferred one on me, so that you may eat and drink at my table in my kingdom and sit on thrones, judging the twelve tribes of Israel" (Luke 22:29–30). We can serve without fear because the kingdom is a gift, not something we earn. From that position of security, we can humble ourselves without any anxiety.

GAME THEORY AND THE GOSPEL

I once heard Andy Crouch comment on the gospel and game theory and our call as followers of Jesus to live sacrificial lives. Game theory is "the branch of mathematics concerned with the analysis of strategies for dealing with competitive situations where the outcome of a participant's choice of action depends critically on the actions of other participants."[8] This hasn't remained in the realm of mathematics or business. It has been used to describe our relationships and culture at large. Game theory can be applied to our interactions and relationships with others like this:

I win; you lose. There are limited resources that we compete for. To get what I want or need, I have to take it from you.

Win-win. This is the modern alternative given in response to such a competitive framework. With a growing awareness of our interconnected world, it seems harsh to care only for the self. But as of late, people have been reflecting on this framework. Though many are willing to help in individual situations, rarely are we willing to change the structural and power dynamics of society to help others. This can result in a sort of paternalism and condescension, even in our best moments of generosity. *Win-win* really means, "I'll help right now if it works, but not if it costs me deeply."

I sacrifice; we win. In this framework, we don't just serve or give to meet an immediate need; we change the posture of our lives to give what we have accumulated in such a way that it costs us something. We sacrifice and serve to raise others up. This third category shakes the structures in which many of us live and calls us into deeper union with the heart of Jesus for the world.

It could not be clearer from Jesus's life that privilege is not something to be ignored or enjoyed. It is to be stewarded for the sake of others. Let Philippians 2:3–8 wash over you with fresh power as you read:

Do nothing out of selfish ambition or vain conceit. Rather, in humility value others above yourselves, not looking to your own interests but each of you to the interests of the others.
    In your relationships with one another, have the same mindset as Christ Jesus:

Who, being in very nature God,
    did not consider equality with God something to be used
        to his own advantage;
rather, he made himself nothing
    by taking the very nature of a servant,
    being made in human likeness.
And being found in appearance as a man,
    he humbled himself
    by becoming obedient to death—
        even death on a cross!

Jesus didn't use his equality with God to his own advantage. He made himself nothing. He took the nature of a servant. He entered this world in humility, so lowly that he embraced public shame and death outside the camp (Hebrews 13:13).

Though we may stand in awe of Jesus doing this on our behalf, it's remarkably hard for those of us raised in the West to follow his example. America is obsessed with winning. We love the direction of "up," the sign of progress. *Up and to the right on the business graph, up and coming, upper class, the upside.* The prospect of progress has brought hope to many people. They are people on the rise. Yet, when progress doesn't happen, we feel robbed.

It's hard for the American church to understand that our cultural privilege isn't just for our enjoyment. We have to redirect the things we possess for the sake of others. The challenge of this, of course, is that our culture hates "down." *Downgrade, downhearted, downsize, downer.* These are the things we avoid like the plague. (Except Down Under, that wonderful slice of heaven on earth!)

Yet Jesus redefined greatness as the distribution of our unearned cultural advantage on behalf of others. Rather than fighting over rights and responsibilities, Jesus calls us to redirect our privilege for others.

There is such potency in sharing the power we have. Redirecting our personal and corporate privilege jams the culture of intersectionality. We read in this passage that Jesus became "obedient to death—even death on a cross!" (Philippians 2:8). This is ultimate intersectionality. God himself entered the world, blocked by sinners, religion, systems, power, and politics. They took hold of the Son of God and crucified him. In a staggering reversal, the public failure of Jesus deconstructs worldly privilege. Now, when people come to God, they come not as winners but as failures. This naturally establishes humility as the basis of our faith. This way, we move through the world with a vision for humbly serving others.

After deconstructing the religious, racial, and gender hierarchies, Jesus made this claim through the apostle Paul: "In Christ Jesus you are all children of God through faith, for all of you who were baptized into Christ have clothed yourselves with Christ. There is neither Jew nor Gentile, neither slave nor free, nor is there male and female, for you are all one in Christ Jesus. If you belong to Christ, then you are Abraham's seed, and heirs according to the promise" (Galatians 3:26–29). In synagogue liturgy, Jewish men prayed this prayer: "Thank you, Lord, that I'm not a woman. Thank you that I'm not a slave. Thank you that I'm not a Gentile." So Paul didn't want followers of Jesus— those saved by the equalizing and redirecting power of the Cross—to step into a system that was upholding harmful hierarchies. By affirming that there is neither Jew nor Gentile, slave nor free, male nor female, one could no longer say these prayers in the synagogue. They were forced to come to terms with the redirection of Christ.[9]

In the church, hierarchies are flattened by the Cross. The church becomes an alternative community. This is cultural subversion, which creates a new humanity in the world. The church should be a place where normal hindrances are removed and all are equal in Jesus. Redirection through the Cross jams the culture of intersectionality.

Chris Arnade had a successful career on Wall Street and was enjoying the comforts of this position. In his moving book *Dignity: Seeking Respect in Back Row America,* he shared the story of his disillusionment with privilege and status and his growing concern for the poor. He spent years traveling around the country, listening to and loving the lost and the least. One thing surprised him again and again in his travels, and it was the presence and persistence of the church in the most broken places in our country. He found that the church was the only place that seemed to treat the addicted and shamed like people; they humanized and loved in profound ways. He wrote, "They say, 'Enter as you are,' letting forgiveness wash away a past that many want gone. You are welcome as long as you try. The churches understand the streets, understand everyone is a sinner and everyone fails. The rest of the world—the courts, the hospitals, the rehab clinics, the welfare office, police stations, and even some of the nonprofits and schools . . . —doesn't understand that. That cold, secular world of the well-intentioned is a distant and judgmental thing."[10]

Distance and judgment—I win; you lose. Welfare and law—win-win. Humanizing compassion and service—I sacrifice; you win.

Servanthood resists privilege, and the kingdom takes root.

THE CHURCH AT ITS BEST

As those imitating Jesus's example, we are called to distribute what we have been given by Jesus to those around us. To those next door, to those in the city, to those in the hardest places on earth. And when Christians embrace this responsibility, we have credibility in the eyes of the world. Nicholas Kristof wrote about this in a *New York Times* article entitled "Evangelicals a Liberal Can Love":

> In parts of Africa where bandits and warlords shoot or rape anything that moves, you often find that the only groups still operating are Doctors Without Borders and religious aid workers: crazy doctors and crazy Christians. In the town of Rutshuru in war-ravaged Congo, I found starving children, raped widows and shellshocked survivors. And there was a determined Catholic nun from Poland, serenely running a church clinic.
>
> Unlike the religious right windbags, she was passionately "pro-life" even for those already born—and brave souls like her are increasingly representative of religious conservatives.[11]

To be clear, it's not so much that those without privilege are being served. Rather, those with privilege are being changed. Their hearts are becoming like Jesus's. Listen to Andy Crouch: "The most transformative acts of our lives are likely to be the moments when we radically empty ourselves, in the very settings where we would normally be expected to exercise authority."[12]

The redirection of our privilege—of which you and I possess incredible amounts—is an opportunity for the church.

So, are you aware of the privilege you have been given? Are you grateful? How has God spoken to you about stewarding it for others? Where do you sense the Spirit leading you? How will you take on the posture of redirection in order to use what you have for others? And how can we as the church create opportunities, in the places God has called us, to be an alternative community, where a group as privileged as us can humble ourselves, sacrifice, and redirect what we have? Privilege isn't a thing to be batted around in politics. It's an opportunity for followers of Jesus to serve our world today. For Jesus, sacrifice was greater than privilege. To follow him well, it must be for us too.

Chapter 9

Celebration Must Resist Cynicism

May the God of hope fill you with all joy and peace as you
trust in him, so that you may overflow with hope by the
power of the Holy Spirit.

Romans 15:13

Sometimes I think the people to feel saddest for are people
who once knew what profoundness was, but who lost or
became numb to the sensation of wonder—people who
closed the doors that lead us into the secret world—or who
had the doors closed for them by time and neglect and
decisions made in times of weakness.

Douglas Coupland, *Life After God*

O ne of the standard characteristics of a true New Yorker is cynicism. In
fact, it's almost impossible to be a New Yorker and not be cynical.
When someone arrives here, full of fresh dreams and excitement, there's a sense
that it's our responsibility to cleanse her of that naive optimism. She stares up
at the skyline and takes in the majesty of the city, and she thinks, *I think I'm
going to do really well here.* And the New Yorker's reply? "I don't know how to

tell you this, but a studio apartment costs $3,000 a month. You're not going to be able to make it here."

Or he walks beneath the flashing lights on Broadway and tells you about all the regional theater he's done, how excited he is to try out for a Broadway production, and the New Yorker says, "Thousands of people move here every year, trying to get into acting. There's no way you're going to make it on Broadway."

Or maybe she has a heart for finance, and she looks down Wall Street with an expression of wonder at the billions of dollars changing hands. But before she even says anything, the New Yorker shakes his head. "It's a brutal city. You're not going to make it in finance."

Cynicism is woven into the fabric of this city. There's something about this place that causes its inhabitants to develop a high level of doubt and skepticism.

But this New York cynicism is just a more obvious version of a deeper cynicism that is leaking into all our hearts. It is moving through our culture like a cancer, and this is a seriously troubling thing because it is a cynicism accompanied by a sense of heavy hopelessness. Even though we live at a time when we are advancing at every technological level and bookshelves and TV shows are flooded with self-help experts telling us how to have incredible lives, our society is crippled by depression, opioid addiction, emptiness, divorce, promiscuity, loneliness, and violence. This cynicism isn't only something conceptual, an emotional idea we talk about and then move on from. It has tangible, real-world effects.

I suppose we could try to fight this deep cynicism by telling positive anecdotes that will make us all feel better, but the challenging part is that, in reality, there is a lot of evidence that the world is a dark, difficult place. All you have to do is watch the world news at night or do a quick Google search on tragedies, and you'll realize that, yes, a lot of bad things do happen in the world. And we don't seem particularly equipped to deal with them.

In the book *Winners Take All,* the author shared the following reasons that cynicism seems like a logical response:

- American scientists make the most important discoveries in medicine and genetics and publish more biomedical research than those of any other country—but the average American's health remains worse and slower-improving than that of peers in other rich countries, and in certain years life expectancy actually declines.
- American inventors create astonishing new ways to learn thanks to the power of video and the Internet, many of them free of charge—but the average twelfth grader tests more poorly in reading today than in 1992.
- The country has had a "culinary renaissance," as one publication puts it, one farmers' market and Whole Foods at a time—but it has failed to improve the nutrition of most people, with the incidence of obesity and related conditions rising over time.
- The tools for becoming an entrepreneur appear to be more accessible than ever, for the student who learns coding online or the Uber driver—but the share of young people who own a business has fallen by two-thirds since the 1980s.
- America has birthed a wildly successful online book superstore called Amazon, and another company, Google, has scanned more than twenty-five million books for public use—but illiteracy has remained stubbornly in place and the fraction of Americans who read at least one work of literature a year has dropped by almost a quarter in recent decades.[1]

We read these kinds of statements, and we wonder, *What's the point? What's the point in taking a risk? What's the point in showing up?*

The problem is that this deep cynicism hasn't become normal just in the culture around us—it is moving into the church. We are cynical about people who show genuine enthusiasm, believing their naivete will be crushed by pain. We are cynical about God moving, because we've witnessed too many unanswered prayers. We are cynical about the possibility of things changing for the better, because we know how hard life can be.

So, instead of being a people who have good news to share, news that could transform the world, we have become a people mired in the twenty-four-hour news cycle, fed a constant diet of hopelessness and despair. Our ability to dismiss the work of God in the church has become toxic. We are plagued by a lack of expectation and have begun to believe that this is all there is.

But the Scriptures declare that God is good, and his goodness should be celebrated. If we slowed down for a minute and broke away from the cynical feeds, every now and then we would be surprised by the work of God in our own lives and the lives of others around us.

Maybe all the bad news is clouding our perspective of what is happening in the world. Maybe we have been trained to pay attention to the darkness and ignore the light. Maybe there is more grace and redemption happening, if we just knew where to look. Maybe we have to learn to identify and celebrate the good and learn to resist a culture of cynicism.

I know it may seem like an interesting juxtaposition—celebration and cynicism. Why not joy resisting cynicism? Or hope resisting cynicism? But *celebration* is explicit. It's defiant. Not only does it recognize who God is and what he is doing, but it also calls for a response. Celebration is godly defiance in a culture of doubt.

We often talk about the spiritual disciplines as a key to our faith. In fact, one of the most popular books on this topic is *Celebration of Discipline.* But could it be that in a cynical world like ours, the key is not the celebration of discipline but the discipline of celebration—making sure we commit to celebrating the good God we serve? I think so.

Celebration resists cynicism.

THE REAL QUESTION

There is a deeper root of this widespread cynicism. We can say we're cynical because life is hard or because the odds are against us, but the real reason for our cynicism is further below the surface, and it comes out of how we answer this question: *What do you think God is like?* If we get this answer wrong, we sow seeds of cynicism in our lives. When we view God as angry or retributive, it will lead us to a cynical view of life. When we believe he is passive, again cynicism.

So, what do you think? Is God happy? Is God in a good mood? Is God filled with joy? If you answered no to those questions, then you won't see those things as being essential to whom we need to be as followers of Christ.

But we do serve a joyful God, and that should make all the difference. Consider these words from John Ortberg:

We will not understand God until we understand this about him:
"God is the happiest being in the universe." God also knows sorrow.
Jesus is remembered, among other things, as "a man of sorrows,
and acquainted with grief." But the sorrow of God, like the anger
of God, is his temporary response to a fallen world. That sorrow will
be banished forever from his heart on the day the world is set right.
Joy is God's basic character. Joy is his eternal destiny. God is the
happiest being in the universe.[2]

Do you believe that? Because if you do—and if you believe you were created in the image of God to represent him to the world—then it's important that you mirror this reality in your life. Things like joy, delight, and celebration are central to our discipline and practice. "Blessed is the people whose God is the LORD" (Psalm 144:15).

Yes, there are sin and suffering in the Bible—and rape and murder and death and violence and heartache—but the Scriptures are the definitive account of God dealing with our sin, not creating it. God is breaking into our hatred and violence and strife with hope and restoration and life. Rather than allowing the lens of cynicism to cloud our view of the Scriptures, we learn to see joy. And when we see the work of God, we celebrate it as a signpost that his kingdom is at hand. Celebrating the goodness of God is a thread throughout Scripture. Celebration, joy, and delight are not subtle hints but dominant themes. God is in a good mood, and he wants the world to know it.

WOVEN INTO THE FABRIC OF CREATION

The first illustration of celebration comes in the first chapter of the Bible, Genesis 1. A lot of us feel anxiety rising as soon as Genesis is mentioned—we're not sure whether we're supposed to be reading it in a scientific way or a poetic way or a literal way. These debates can sometimes paralyze our ability to see what is going on. The dominant theme is a good God creating out of joy and delight. There's one statement used over and over in Genesis 1: "God saw that it was good." Again and again and again, God created something new, and again and again and again, he confirmed that what he created was good.

We're given an even deeper insight into how God viewed his creation in Job 38:

> Where were you when I laid the earth's foundation?
>   Tell me, if you understand.
> Who marked off its dimensions? Surely you know!
>   Who stretched a measuring line across it?
> On what were its footings set,
>   or who laid its cornerstone—
> while the morning stars sang together
>   and all the angels shouted for joy? (verses 4–7)

What was going on while God was busy creating? The morning stars were singing together and the angels were shouting for joy. This was the soundtrack for creation. God wasn't sitting there in stoic reserve, shaping creation with a disapproving eye. No, the stars were singing and the angels were shouting for joy. There was a heartbeat pulsing through the universe as God was creating, and that heartbeat was pounding out the same words over and over.

It is good.

It is good.

It is good.

God's heart was in it, and an enormous outflow of celebration surrounded it. If we carefully tune our ears, we can still hear the echo of the angels' shouts today.

CELEBRATING GENEROSITY

One area Christians approach with a sense of obligation (and often cynicism) is tithing. How many of us, when we're about to give to the Lord, think, *Here they go again—all they want is my money*? But could it be that God wants to liberate us from the tyranny of greed by celebrating generosity? Deuteronomy 14 introduces this idea:

> Be sure to set aside a tenth of all that your fields produce each year. Eat the tithe of your grain, new wine and olive oil, and the firstborn of your herds and flocks in the presence of the LORD your God at the place he will choose as a dwelling for his Name, so that you may learn to revere the LORD your God always. But if that place is too distant and you have been blessed by the LORD your God and cannot carry your tithe (because the place where the LORD will choose to put his Name is so far away), then exchange your tithe for silver, and take the silver with you and go to the place the LORD your God will choose. Use the silver

to buy whatever you like: cattle, sheep, wine or other fermented drink, or anything you wish. Then you and your household shall eat there in the presence of the LORD your God and rejoice. (verses 22–26)

Do you discern what's taking place here? God is inviting his people into the privilege of giving, all the while making a case for celebration. It's right there in the text. If you have to travel too far with your tithe, then exchange the tithe for silver, and when you arrive at the specified place, use that silver to buy "whatever you like: cattle, sheep, wine or other fermented drink, or anything you wish." Then go ahead and celebrate. This is a vision of bourbon and barbecue. Fermented drink and fatty meat. "You and your household shall eat there in the presence of the LORD your God and rejoice."

What if we approached our opportunity to give as an invitation from God into a space of celebration? What if the sound of our rejoicing at the chance to give could be heard from a long way off? What if people standing outside the churches in this country heard laughter and singing and the sounds of excitement and turned to one another to say, "They must be collecting the offering"?

CELEBRATING TRUTH

Many of us have been trained to think of the Bible as an oppressive book. Reading it in our modern context can raise questions and suspicions about life under its authority. Does it really carry good news? But time and again we read of celebration being a response to the revelation of the Word.

One of the clearest accounts of this is in Nehemiah. After the children of Israel finished rebuilding the wall and gates of Jerusalem, they listened to Ezra read the Word of the Lord.

Nehemiah, who was the governor, and Ezra the priest and scribe, and the Levites who taught the people said to all the people, "This

day is holy to the LORD your God; do not mourn or weep." For all
the people wept as they heard the words of the Law. Then he said
to them, "Go your way. Eat the fat and drink sweet wine and send
portions to anyone who has nothing ready, for this day is holy to
our Lord. And do not be grieved, for the joy of the LORD is your
strength." So the Levites calmed all the people, saying, "Be quiet,
for this day is holy; do not be grieved." And all the people went
their way to eat and drink and to send portions and to make great
rejoicing, because they had understood the words that were declared
to them. (8:9–12, ESV)

Revelation led to rejoicing, great rejoicing. (When is the last time you left
a Bible study doing that?) What a vision! Rejoicing arose at the rediscovery of
the Word. Not the sound of weeping and despair, not the sound of lamentation
and regret, but the sound of celebration.

I once met a longtime New Yorker who asked what I did. When I told her
I was a pastor, she asked whether I was "from that large happy-clappy church
in the city."

" 'Happy-clappy'?" I asked.

"The one with all the singing and dancing and joy," she said.

I had to confess I didn't work at that church, but the thought stuck in my
mind for days. What a reputation! Though she knew almost nothing about
faith, there was a community defined by joy whose reputation preceded it. And
though I wasn't a part of it, I wanted to be.

Again and again in the Old Testament, we find that God's presence is
something to be celebrated, not tolerated. Whether it's David dancing before
the Lord with all his might in the presence of a cynical wife (2 Samuel 6:14–
16), the major festivals that basically functioned like the Coachella of the ancient Near East, or the calls for celebration in the Psalms, joy was to be a feature
of the covenant people of God.

JUBILEE

Imagine being a child and your family has had a rough couple of decades and you ache for change. You feel frustration and angst. But this is not the defining story of your life, because you know that Jubilee is coming. In every age there will be a horizon of hope despite the despair.

"Is it Jubilee yet, Dad?"

"No, only three more years."

"Is it Jubilee yet, Dad?"

"No, only two more years. Trust me—the whole world will know when Jubilee arrives."

And when Jubilee finally arrives, there are freedom and joy and a celebration unlike any other. Forgiveness, restoration, reparation, and return. A one-year rest that reminds the nation what life is like under the goodness of God.

JESUS AND THE CYNICS

One of the Enemy's chief goals has always been to question the goodness of God. To get us to believe that freedom and life are found apart from God, not with him (Genesis 3:1–5). "Did God really say?" is the lie behind all other lies.

To settle this debate, the Father sent his Son into the world to introduce jubilee as a counterculture on this planet. The whole narrative of Jesus's arrival is framed as a celebration. The angels said they brought "good news of great joy" (Luke 2:10, ESV). Later, when Jesus began his ministry, he set it up theologically under the theme of celebration.

He stood up to read, and the scroll of the prophet Isaiah was handed to him. Unrolling it, he found the place where it is written:

"The Spirit of the Lord is on me,
    because he has anointed me

to proclaim good news to the poor.
He has sent me to proclaim freedom for the prisoners
and recovery of sight for the blind,
to set the oppressed free,
to proclaim the year of the Lord's favor."

Then he rolled up the scroll, gave it back to the attendant and sat down. The eyes of everyone in the synagogue were fastened on him. He began by saying to them, "Today this scripture is fulfilled in your hearing." (Luke 4:16–21)

"To proclaim the year of the Lord's favor"—this is why Jesus came. He wanted not a year of Jubilee but a culture of jubilee. His whole ministry was to be defined as a celebration of our redemption and restoration by God. Surprisingly, the audience didn't take this news too well. Jesus had to contend with the cynics of his day to establish a culture of celebration. In this encounter, rather than receiving his message, they sought to throw him off a cliff (verses 28–29). Celebration in a world of cynics is something that must be fought for.

Regardless of that response, Jesus went on to proclaim God's invitation to redemption and celebration. Jesus sought out those who had been excluded by cynical religion and invited them back home. This theme of celebration dominates Jesus's parables.

In Luke 14, he told the story of a man who decides to have a great banquet and invites many to join him (verses 16–24). When the preparations are made, he sends out his servant to gather those who were invited, yet some refuse to come. His servant returns, bearing all the excuses of the guests who will not attend. One said he had bought a field and had to go see it. Another said he had recently purchased five yoke of oxen and had to inspect them. Another said he was married and couldn't make it. It was the normal stuff of life that got in the way of the celebration of God.

When the servant gives this news, the host of the banquet grows furious.

But instead of simmering in an empty banquet hall, he sends his servant out to bring in guests from the city: the poor, the crippled, the lame, and the blind. The servant does all this, comes back, and lets him know there is still room for more. So he sends the servant out again to the highways and lanes outside the city to bring in anyone he finds. God wants the house to be full, the celebration to be great.

Have you ever been to a party where the place was packed, the music loud, the people laughing and thrilled to be together? The amount of energy and excitement in an environment like that is overwhelming. What a party! What life! And in Jesus's ministry, those on the margins were reveling in it with passion and joy.

In the very next chapter of Luke, Jesus hammered home the same point. In fact, he told three stories back to back to cement the theme in his listeners' minds.

Luke 15 begins,

> Now the tax collectors and sinners were all gathering around to hear
> Jesus. But the Pharisees and the teachers of the law muttered, "This
> man welcomes sinners and eats with them."
>   Then Jesus told them this parable . . . (verses 1–3)

Jesus told the story of a man who has one hundred sheep. One of them goes missing, so he leaves the ninety-nine in the open field and sets out to find the one. When he recovers the lost sheep, he celebrates and returns home. "Then he calls his friends and neighbors together and says, 'Rejoice with me; I have found my lost sheep'" (verse 6). Jesus stated, "There will be more rejoicing in heaven over one sinner who repents than over ninety-nine righteous persons who do not need to repent" (verse 7).

From there he moved to a story of a woman who loses a valuable coin. She lights a lamp, sweeps the house, and searches diligently until she finds it. Once she finally recovers it, does she place it in her pocket and go on with her day as if nothing has happened? No! She gathers her neighbors and says, "Rejoice with me; I have found my lost coin" (verse 9).

The third story in this trio of parables is that of the prodigal son. The younger son runs away, spends his money on prostitutes and wild living, and heads home in shame and need. But when his father sees him coming from "a long way off" (verse 20), he runs down the road, cuts off the young man's repentance speech, and prepares a feast to celebrate his return.

The older brother comes in from the field where he was working and hears the party. He's angry, and he confronts his father, asking where his party is. Why wasn't he, the responsible one, ever allowed to celebrate? But his father says, "Everything I have is yours" (verse 31). The older brother failed to realize the culture of his own house. His cynicism shut him out of his own celebration. Cynics in every age miss what is available to them.

Jesus insisted that the work of God demands celebration. He is in the world, bringing good news, welcoming the outsider, restoring the lost, binding up the broken. The question is, Will we join the feast or issue excuses?

WIRED TO CELEBRATE

Modern science continues to help us understand how the brain regulates moods and emotions. It even reveals a kind of plasticity enabling our brains to change when certain behaviors are repeated. We know this is true for some forms of addiction (such as viewing pornography), but did you know this works in the area of celebration? Neurobiologists have shown that while the majority of the brain's development stops during childhood, there is one location in the right orbital prefrontal cortex that has the ability to grow throughout your life. This has been called the "joy center." One book's authors observed, "When the joy center has been sufficiently developed, it regulates emotions, pain control and immunity centers; it guides us to act like ourselves; it releases neurotransmitters like dopamine and serotonin; and it is the only part of the brain that overrides the main drive centers—food and sexual impulses, terror and rage."[3] Without sufficient "joy strength," we spend our lives trying to fill the deficit.

The practice of celebration strengthens this part of our brains. Unlike hedonism, which requires increasing amounts of pleasure for decreasing reward, celebration strengthens the joy center, which transforms our entire outlook. Hope is contagious. Giving thanks is contagious. So, how can you begin to resist cynicism and build a culture of celebration for yourself?

PERSONAL CELEBRATION

We need to begin by cultivating personal celebration in our lives. Marking key moments of God's goodness can reframe our entire stories.

I have always been inspired by the way Blaise Pascal marked his moment of redemption. On November 23, 1654, he had an overwhelming encounter with God that shaped the rest of his life. He wrote,

From about half past ten in the evening until about half past twelve,

FIRE

God of Abraham, God of Isaac, God of Jacob, not of the philosophers
    and scholars.
Certitude. Certitude. Feeling. Joy. Peace.
God of Jesus Christ
Deum meum et Deum vestrum.
"Your God shall be my God."
Forgetfulness of the world and of everything else, except God.
    He is to be found only by the ways taught in the Gospel.
    Greatness of the human soul.
    "Righteous Father, the world has not known You, but I have known You."
    Joy, joy, joy, tears of joy.[4]

After his death, this account was found sewn into his coat, a daily reminder and filter of his experience of life.

We would do well to follow Pascal's example. We often talk about the church calendar (Advent, Christmas, Epiphany, Lent, and so on), but what about crafting your own redemptive calendar? We can build our own rhythms of celebration that declare the goodness of God to those who know us best. Celebration would become personal; rejoicing, tangible.

I was at a prayer meeting recently when I overheard a woman in our congregation use a curious phrase. "This is my one-year spiritual birthday," Meghan said.

I was struck by the thought. What a delightful thing to say! We each have a regular birthday, the date of which we did not choose, but spiritual birthdays are different. This day is the one on which we encountered forgiveness. One we choose to celebrate.

Meghan shared some of the ways her life has been changed during her first year of redemption.

Here's a list of some of the incredible things Jesus has done in my year of walking with him (yay for spiritual birthdays!) . . .

- Jesus has completely redeemed and restored my relationship with my dad. We had a very shallow relationship, due to years of wounds and harsh remarks. Today, my dad is one of my most life-giving sources. We constantly share Scripture, Christian podcasts, and worship music with each other and talk about what Jesus is doing in our daily lives. He listens to our church's podcast every Wednesday morning, so we can discuss what I am learning in my community.

- God's plan and provision for my life is becoming more revealed to me every day. In my season of freelancing, God's hand is so clear. Most of my work comes from members of our community, who I didn't even know a little over a year ago. In April, when I was let go

from my job, if I didn't know Jesus, I know that I would have left
NYC. He has so graciously given me a community to love me and
encourage me to grow in my knowledge of him during this season.
He has also restored the burnout I had from corporate life and
given me new vision and creativity.

- Creation is my sacred pathway and God talks to me every day
  through sunrises, sunsets, and the sky. Even in the chaos of NYC,
  he gives me little signs of his love everywhere and every day, where
  I can't help but to stop and praise him.
- There was a sin that I struggled with for years and one that caused
  a lot of brokenness and pain in my life. After surrendering that area
  of my life to Jesus in April, he has completely removed all temptation and desire from my life and replaced it with a desire to know
  him and spend more time with him.

Imagine going into a house for a party and realizing this is one of the liveli-
est celebrations you've ever attended. There's good food and the people are
friendly. Everyone seems excited to be there. You find the host and ask her,
"What are we celebrating?" and the host says, "We're celebrating my ninth year
of being a Christian!" Imagine if we had entire parties where the only reason
for the party was to recount the mercy of God and his powerful work in your
life. I think even our most cynical friends would be drawn to a faith like that.

COMMUNAL CELEBRATION

Richard Foster wrote, "The decision to set the mind on the higher things of life
is an act of the will. That is why celebration is a Discipline. It is not something
that falls on our heads. It is the result of a consciously chosen way of thinking
and living. When we choose this way, the healing and redemption in Christ
will break into the inner recesses of our lives and relationships, and the inevitable result will be joy."[5]

The local church communities we are part of need to put the good news of Jesus at the center of our lives. We must learn to choose this way of thinking and living. We need to be known for more than creedal adherence, service of the poor, and convictions about biblical ethics. We need to be known as those who know how to celebrate and party. Those with instincts of joy who seize the moments and mark redemption. Who order desserts, raise glasses high, create space for sharing the work of God, and root it all in his goodness.

The more we practice the discipline of celebration, the more it will become our instinct. Instead of passing over moments of grace and redemption, we will mark them, and hope and love will seep into our cynical world.

And this kind of joy is infectious. "In the New Testament," one campus minister pointed out, "the Greek word *skirtáo* is used to describe this joy. It means literally to leap or spring about as a sign of joy. It was used of the infant John the Baptist, who 'leaped for joy' in his mother's womb at the arrival of Mary, the expectant mother of Jesus. It occurs again in the words of Jesus to followers who encounter persecution for his sake: 'Rejoice in that day, and *leap for joy*, for behold, your reward is great in heaven; for so their fathers did to the prophets.'"[6] Learning to leap as an instinct of joy—what a picture! Maybe you can be the one who leads in changing the culture of your community. Maybe the spirit of joy within you will recognize the work around you and hope will begin to rise.

I was at one of these redemption celebrations with a group of my friends not long ago. A crew of us from the city were gathered around a table, reveling in all God had done. Person by person, we opened our hearts and shared God's goodness. We laughed till it hurt, wept tears of gratitude, and ate until we were content. People shared freedom from sexual addiction, deliverance from a judgmental spirit, reconciled relationships with family, promotions at work, and fresh hope in a strained marriage. At the end of the meal, we all raised our glasses and yelled, "To the King and to the kingdom!" The whole restaurant turned around for a second, drawn into the spirit of the moment. Later the server, who had caught snippets of our stories, said to me, "That was the most hopeful thing I have encountered in years, and I don't even believe in God. Thank you."

Cynicism is killing our nation. It's destroying our hearts. It's putting us in a place where we cannot appreciate the joy that comes from this good news we have been given. But God has an antidote to cynicism—his presence, his redemption, and his fullness of joy. When we take time to celebrate, whether personally or communally, we are bringing the glory of God into the brokenness of the world around us. We're accurately representing the God we serve and offering tangible grace to the world. As Paul so perfectly wrote, "May the God of hope fill you with all joy and peace as you trust in him, so that you may overflow with hope by the power of the Holy Spirit" (Romans 15:13). May celebration overflow in your life and resist the cynicism we face today.

Epilogue

It's early in the morning and I am drinking coffee, trying to keep my eyes open after a subway ride. I am in New York, where I speak the language, understand the street signs, and know exactly where I am going. I am revisiting a season from the life of Dietrich Bonhoeffer that has haunted my pastoral ministry for as long as I can remember.

I get off the 1 train at 125th, walk up the hill, and slowly draw to a stop. The air is warm; the day is quiet—not much in sight. There are no historical markers, no signs of what I am looking for, so I slowly move toward the front of a deli to reflect.

As hard as it is for me to believe, I have been a pastor in New York for almost fifteen years. I moved here in my twenties with a vision to start a church. I was full of faith and naivete and idealism—all the things that make you leave a comfortable life at a megachurch in the suburbs, sell all your possessions, pay off another's debts as they did in the book of Acts (2:44–45), and start from scratch. These years have been filled with the most brutal and beautiful moments of my life. In following Jesus in New York, my church and I have laughed together, wept together, screamed at one another, broken bread and drunk wine in forgiveness, and sat stunned at the tangible grace of God in our midst. We have also been slandered and misunderstood, have experienced betrayal and accusation almost more than we can bear. And as of late, to be honest, these years seem to have taken a toll. I have asked God for an easier call. I have had a desire that I can't ignore to go someplace else. Somewhere less secular, somewhere less transient. Somewhere the walk with Jesus is downhill. As these thoughts run through my mind, I unconsciously let out a deep sigh.

BONHOEFFER IN NEW YORK

Bonhoeffer left Germany for New York by steamship on September 6, 1930. Little more than a month earlier, he had given his first lecture in Berlin after qualifying to be a lecturer by submitting his second postdoctoral thesis at the age of twenty-four. Bonhoeffer came to study theology at Union Theological Seminary, which served as an illuminating experience of the American seminarian, though as a doctorate-holding graduate of Berlin University who had studied under the leading theologians in the world, this experience was academically lackluster for him. He was equally disappointed in the church of the day.

> In New York, they preach about virtually everything; only one thing is
> not addressed, or is addressed so rarely that I have as yet been unable
> to hear it, namely, the gospel of Jesus Christ. . . . So what stands in
> place of the Christian message? An ethical and social idealism borne
> by a faith in progress that—who knows how—claims the right to call
> itself "Christian." And in the place of the church as the congregation
> of believers in Christ there stands the church as a social corporation.
> Anyone who has seen the weekly program of one of the large New
> York churches, with their daily, indeed almost hourly events . . .
> anyone who has become acquainted with the embarrassing nervous-
> ness with which the pastor lobbies for membership—that person can
> well assess the character of such a church. . . .
>
> In order to balance out the feeling of inner emptiness that arises
> now and then (and partly also to refill the church's treasury), some
> congregations will if possible engage an evangelist for a "revival" once
> a year.[1]

He went on, "The church is really no longer the place where the congregation hears and preaches God's word, but rather the place where one acquires secondary significance as a social entity for this or that purpose."[2]

Though the church left much to be desired, Bonhoeffer loved New York. He was metropolitan to the core, and the city offered his endless appetite a smorgasbord of experiences. Bonhoeffer wrote to Max Diestel, his church superintendent back home in Germany, "If you really try to experience New York completely, it almost does you in."[3]

The only genuine expression of the Christian faith that Bonhoeffer experienced in America was in the "negro churches."[4] Longing to escape the shadow of the liberal powerhouse Riverside, pastored by the hyperliberal Harry Emerson Fosdick, Bonhoeffer was overjoyed to attend Abyssinian Baptist Church with his African American friend Albert Franklin "Frank" Fisher. The preacher, Dr. Adam Clayton Powell Sr., who was the son of slaves, had once been given over to vice but came to know Jesus in 1885. One author described Bonhoeffer's experience: "Starving from the skim milk at Union, Bonhoeffer found [at Abyssinian] a theological feast that spared nothing. Powell combined the fire of a revivalist preacher with great intellect and social vision. He was active in combating racism and minced no words about the saving power of Jesus Christ. He didn't fall for the Hobson's choice of one or the other; he believed that without both, one had neither, but with both, one had everything and more."[5] Bonhoeffer reveled in the worship and the Word. "In contrast to the often lecturelike character of the 'white' sermon, the 'black Christ' is preached with captivating passion and vividness. Anyone who has heard and understood the Negro spirituals knows about [their] strange mixture of reserved melancholy and eruptive joy."[6] Bonhoeffer would later include these songs in worship at Finkenwalde, perhaps one of the first places in Europe such songs were used.

On June 20, 1931, Bonhoeffer returned to Germany aboard a steamer. He was inspired by the Jesus he met in Harlem and the power of the African American church. It gave him much fuel for resistance among the Nazis and deep vision for the power and possibility of Finkenwalde.

"I Am Thine"

Fast-forward several years to April 1938. This was a tragic month for Bonhoeffer. Some of the Confessing Church pastors, to avoid losing their careers, took the oath of allegiance to the Führer. Bonhoeffer began to despair of the resistance and fell into a deep depression. Shortly after came Kristallnacht, the night of broken glass. Jewish businesses were destroyed, and all those who dissented were threatened with punishment or—even worse—death. Overwhelmed and unsure of what to do next, Bonhoeffer in the summer of 1939 took a steamer back to Manhattan and the security of New York. What could one man do in the midst of the powers on the rise? But his conscience would not rest easy. His former love for the culture and richness of New York faded. It all became bland and trivial, and the need for faith in his homeland overtook his heart. He knew he could not stay. He had to fight for the gospel amid the compromise of the Reich. He had to contend for the future of the German church. Cause had to be more compelling than comfort. Mission than safety. He had to resist.

In a letter to theologian Reinhold Niebuhr, he gave the following explanation:

> I have made a mistake in coming to America. I must live through this
> difficult period of our national history with the Christian people of
> Germany. I will have no right to participate in the reconstruction
> of Christian life in Germany after the war if I do not share the trials
> of this time with my people. . . . Christians in Germany will face the
> terrible alternative of either willing the defeat of their nation in order
> that Christian civilization may survive, or willing the victory of their
> nation and thereby destroying civilization. I know which of these
> alternatives I must choose; but I cannot make this choice in security.[7]

Bonhoeffer returned home—a decision that would ultimately cost his life. Imprisoned in 1943 for his participation in a plot to destroy Hitler, he spent his time writing, comforting others, resisting as he knew how. On April 9, 1945, Bonhoeffer was executed at Flossenbürg concentration camp. He was thirty-nine years old. Shortly afterward, the camp was liberated.

Before his death, he wrote a poem touching on the themes he was wrestling with. But the final line is the one that stirs hope: "I am thine." Bonhoeffer knew that life was stronger than death, resurrection stronger than the grave, his identity as a son stronger than his designation as a traitor. He wrote,

Who am I? They often tell me
I would step from my cell's confinement
calmly, cheerfully, firmly,
like a squire from his country-house.

Who am I? They often tell me
I would talk to my warders
freely and friendly and clearly,
as though it were mine to command.

Who am I? They also tell me
I would bear the days of misfortune
equably, smilingly, proudly,
like one accustomed to win.

Am I then really all that which other men tell of?
Or am I only what I know of myself,
restless and longing and sick, like a bird in a cage,
struggling for breath, as though hands were compressing my throat,
yearning for colours, for flowers, for the voices of birds,
thirsting for words of kindness, for neighbourliness,
trembling with anger at despotisms and petty humiliation,
tossing in expectation of great events,

powerlessly trembling for friends at an infinite distance,
weary and empty at praying, at thinking, at making,
faint, and ready to say farewell to it all?

Who am I? This or the other?
Am I one person today, and tomorrow another?
Am I both at once? A hypocrite before others,
and before myself a contemptibly woebegone weakling?
Or is something within me still like a beaten army,
fleeing in disorder from victory already achieved?

Who am I? They mock me, these lonely questions of mine.
Whoever I am, thou knowest, O God, I am thine.[8]

A BEAUTIFUL RESISTANCE

I'm sure that you have felt that same desire to escape the drama of the church
in our modern life of faith. At night you probably have deep questions about
whether staying involved is worth it. Worth the misunderstanding, worth the
heartache, worth the credibility hits, worth the sacrifice. And I am sure that
some around you have come to the conclusion that it is not. They have wavered
and shrunk back, preferring spirituality over religion, and given up on the institution known as the church. Maybe you are reading this at a time when you
are struggling to see the point of the church when she is stained by so much
compromise. Maybe you would like to retreat to that easier place of spirituality
without religion. But I'm guessing that deep down in your heart you actually
long for more.

Bailing on commitment rarely leads to renewal; it often leads only to more
cynicism. God can use the tension and angst you feel for good. For reform, for
restoration, and for hope. And this isn't at some cosmic level that you never

personally witness. It can happen in your heart, your life, and your community. You can start as a counterculture of one to push back darkness and seek the light. To start your own beautiful resistance.

How would things change if you resolved to rebel against your own indifference and embody the things you long to see in the world? If you resolved that you would pursue beauty and resist brokenness? That you would resist idolatry with worship, exhaustion with rest, apathy with hunger, fear with hospitality, contempt with honor, hate with love, privilege with sacrifice, and cynicism with celebration? If your life became a parable of what happens when someone lives with integrity and in community no matter the cost?

God is looking for people to live this way, in spite of the hopelessness around them. Those he can use to inspire others, those who pursue his pleasure in a culture of compromise. Will you respond to that call?

I'M STILL HERE

I take the train back to the building in which I live. I climb the steps to the roof overlooking the city. I reflect deeply on Bonhoeffer's choice to return to Germany and flee the safety he encountered in America. Despite all he had seen, his disappointment with the closing of Finkenwalde, the compromise of his friends, and the danger ahead. Yet he believed in the gospel; he believed in the church. He believed in Christ and his kingdom and that it was worth giving his life for. I must have been there for some time, staring out as I do. I didn't hear my daughter come up behind me. She put her arms around my waist. "You look so intense, Dad. What are you thinking about?" So I told her.

That our lives have to count for something. That the church can be a thing of beauty. That at times things are hard and my faith falters but I sense the hunger to press on. "What am I thinking?" I eventually say. "I am thinking *this*"—pointing to our church—"must resist *that*"—painting the outline of the city with my hand.

Study Guide

This guide includes activities, discussion questions, and reflection questions for each chapter in *Beautiful Resistance*. Before each group session, read the related chapter and then do step 1 ("Individual Activity") on your own. During the session, go to step 2 ("Group Discussion") and talk through the questions with the other group members. Finally, after the session, do step 3 ("Reflection") on your own to personalize the impact of what you've been discussing.

    Join the resistance!

Session 1

Introduction / A Church Coming Back to Life

In the introduction, Jon shared about Dietrich Bonhoeffer contrasting the power of the Third Reich with the power of his seminary, highlighting the need for discipleship and Christian formation. Bonhoeffer believed the forces of the Reich were competing for the allegiance of God's people and had to be resisted. Jon's point is that we face much the same situation today.

"We live in a time," he said, "when the church is compromising with the culture left, right, and center, and we're losing our influence. Though there is no specific 'Hitler' pressuring us, we face a myriad of forces seeking to sabotage our faith. Because of the tectonic shift in sexuality, ethics, technology, secular ideologies, religion, and globalization, much of the familiar landscape has been swept away."

In the first chapter, he added, "The church that Jesus founded on his compassion and grace has at times failed to even resemble its founder. Celebrity pastor scandals; abuses in the Catholic Church; political hijacking; indifference to the humanitarian crises of our day, including refugees, racism, and environmentalism; materialism; and complacency have caused many to leave the church."

It's a grim picture Jon painted. But he also held out hope that the church, as Jesus Christ designed it, is still alive and can learn once again to resist pressures in the culture.

BEFORE THE SESSION

Step 1: Individual Activity

Spend a few minutes on your favorite social media site, one of the major news websites, and maybe also a Christian news website. As you do so, think critically about what you are seeing and what it says about our culture and today's church.

How does the information you see on the websites reveal brokenness in society? That is, How do you see evidence of such things as these?

- conflict and violence
- hate and disrespect
- greed
- a debased view of human life
- indifference to suffering

What do you see that reveals Christians justifying sin or participating in ungodly trends in the culture?

DURING THE SESSION

Step 2: Group Discussion

1. What was your experience of church growing up? How has that changed as an adult?

2. What have been your most beautiful moments with the church? How did those moments shape you?

3. What have been the most broken moments with the church? How did those moments affect you?

4. How have you responded to these experiences?

5. Is your view of the church optimistic or pessimistic? Do you have high trust or low trust?

6. What are the dominant forces in the world today that we must resist as faithful followers of Jesus?

7. Where do you see these forces at work?

8. Do you see any of these forces pressuring your life?

9. What feelings do these observations provoke in you?

10. Jon discussed three biblical metaphors for the church that directly contrast with the brokenness of the church: (1) the bride, (2) the temple, and (3) the body. Which metaphor do you most resonate with and find most hopeful? Why?

11. How would you like to see the church act differently in response to harmful trends?

12. What kinds of changes do you personally think you need to make to be a part of the "new resistance" to anti-Christian and antibiblical influences in society?

AFTER THE SESSION

Step 3: Reflection

List all the churches you have attended.

How did they help you? How did they hurt you? What did they teach you?

How have they shaped your vision for what is means to "be" the church?

List one thing you are grateful for about each of the spiritual leaders you've been under. Spend time praying for each of them, that God will guide, guard, and strengthen them. Also, spend time praying for your current church, for protection, vision, and integrity. Ask God to show you how you can be a light for the full biblical message in your church and community.

Session 2

Worship Must Resist Idolatry

Bruce Ellis Benson wrote,

> Not only are we capable of creating idols and worshiping them, we are
> likewise capable of being almost or completely blind to their existence.
> Worse yet, we are often quite capable of providing a defense (and
> sometimes a remarkably respectable defense) for why our particular
> idols are worthy and even orthodox. Our recognition of idols for what
> they are is often selective. Most of us have reasonably well developed
> idol-detectors when it comes to the idols of others. Yet it is probably
> safe to say that all of us have our own particular repertoire of idols.[1]

In chapter 2, Jon helped us consider what we're placing in the position that
only God should occupy. Our culture has plenty of things that it idolizes. We
need to be people who reject the idols of career, sex, or whatever has taken the
place of God.

BEFORE THE SESSION

Step 1: Individual Activity
Take some time on your own this week and ask God to search your heart. Get
in a quiet place and invite the Holy Spirit to come and speak to you. Begin by
praying Psalm 139:23–24 and offering yourself to God.

Search me, God, and know my heart;
   test me and know my anxious thoughts.
See if there is any offensive way in me,
   and lead me in the way everlasting.

Then spend some time thinking through several of these questions in the presence of the Holy Spirit. Ask him for insight.

What makes you tick? What sun does your planet revolve around? What do you organize your life around?

Where do you find safety, comfort, escape, and pleasure? What or whom do you trust?

Whose performance matters? On whose shoulders does the well-being of your world rest? Who can make it better, make it work, make it safe, make it successful?

Whom must you please? Whose opinion of you counts? From whom do you desire approval and fear rejection?

On your deathbed, what will sum up your life? What gives your life meaning?

What would bring you the greatest pleasure or happiness? The greatest pain or misery?

What do you see as your rights? What do you feel entitled to?

When you are pressured, where do you turn? What do you think about? What are your escapes? What do you escape from?

What do you think about most often? What preoccupies or absorbs you? In the morning, to what does your mind drift instinctively?

What are your characteristic fantasies—those that either bring you pleasure or cause fear? What do you daydream about? What do your night dreams revolve around?

Where do you find your identity? How do you define who you are?

DURING THE SESSION

Step 2: Group Discussion

1. Are you aware of a time in your life when you were caught up in idolatry? What was it?

2. How did it affect you? How did you break free?

3. What do you think are the dominant *heart* idols (see pages 28–29) that affect people in your community?

4. What do you think are the dominant *cultural* idols (see pages 29–31) that affect people in your city?

5. How do these idols lie to us about our identity, significance, and worth?

6. How do you know if something you want is turning into an idol?

7. How can good things (e.g., family, relationships, work, love) become idols?

8. Jon mentioned that idols wreak havoc on our lives the following ways: deception, distortion, and destruction (pages 33–36). How is this damage happening around you through a cultural idol?

9. How is this damage happening around you through a heart idol?

10. What have you learned from your own experience about surrendering idolatry and turning back to God?

AFTER THE SESSION

Step 3: Reflection

In order for idolatry to be resisted, it must be recognized and replaced. There is no better way of doing this than fixing our gaze on the power and beauty of God.

Look over this list of the attributes of God. Pick out the ones that stand out to you the most. Then begin to worship God for what each of those reveals to you, and declare its power over the lies of all idols.

1. *God is infinite—he is self-existing, without origin.*

He is before all things, and in him all things hold together.
(Colossians 1:17)

Great is our Lord, and abundant in power;
his understanding is beyond measure.
(Psalm 147:5, ESV)

2. *God is immutable—he never changes.*

I the LORD do not change. (Malachi 3:6)

3. *God is self-sufficient—he has no needs.*

As the Father has life in himself, so he has granted
the Son also to have life in himself. (John 5:26)

4. *God is omnipotent—he is all-powerful.*

By the word of the LORD the heavens were made,
their starry host by the breath of his mouth.
(Psalm 33:6)

5. *God is omniscient—he is all-knowing.*

Remember the former things, those of long ago;
I am God, and there is no other;
I am God, and there is none like me.
I make known the end from the beginning,
from ancient times, what is still to come.

I say, "My purpose will stand,
  and I will do all that I please." (Isaiah 46:9–10)

6. *God is omnipresent—he is always everywhere.*

Where can I go from Your Spirit?
Or where can I flee from Your presence?
If I ascend to heaven, You are there;
If I make my bed in Sheol, behold, You are there.
If I take the wings of the dawn,
If I dwell in the remotest part of the sea,
Even there Your hand will lead me,
And Your right hand will lay hold of me.
  (Psalm 139:7–10, NASB)

7. *God is wise—he is full of perfect, unchanging wisdom.*

Oh, the depth of the riches both of the wisdom and knowledge of God! How unsearchable are His judgments and unfathomable His ways! (Romans 11:33, NASB)

8. *God is faithful—he is infinitely, unchangingly true.*

Know therefore that the LORD your God is God; he is the faithful God, keeping his covenant of love to a thousand generations of those who love him and keep his commandments. (Deuteronomy 7:9)

9. *God is good—he is infinitely, unchangingly full of goodwill.*

O taste and see that the LORD is good. (Psalm 34:8, NASB)

10. *God is just—he is infinitely, unchangingly right in all he does.*

The Rock! His work is perfect,
For all His ways are just;
A God of faithfulness and without injustice,
Righteous and upright is He. (Deuteronomy 32:4, NASB)

11. *God is merciful—he is infinitely, unchangingly compassionate and kind.*

"I will have mercy on whom I have mercy, and I will have
compassion on whom I have compassion." So then it does
not depend on the man who wills or the man who runs,
but on God who has mercy. (Romans 9:15–16, NASB)

12. *God is gracious—he longs to have compassion on us.*

The LORD is gracious and merciful;
Slow to anger and great in lovingkindness. (Psalm 145:8, NASB)

13. *God is loving—he infinitely, unchangingly loves us.*

Dear friends, let us love one another, for love comes
from God. Everyone who loves has been born of God
and knows God. Whoever does not love does not know
God, because God is love. (1 John 4:7–8)

14. *God is holy—he is infinitely, unchangingly perfect.*

Holy, holy, holy is the Lord God Almighty. (Revelation 4:8)

15. *God is glorious—he is infinitely beautiful and great.*

> His radiance is like the sunlight;
> He has rays flashing from His hand,
> And there is the hiding of His power. (Habakkuk 3:4, NASB)

Session 3

Rest Must Resist Exhaustion

Many of us feel overwhelmed and burnt out. We feel that we have lost control of our lives, careers, and souls because of the relentless pace of modern life. This poses a real threat to our formation and devotion as followers of Jesus. We are at risk of being more shaped by a secular pace than a sacred one. Many of us wonder how we can get in touch with the deeper longings of our hearts and learn to enjoy God and the gift of life in the midst of so much relentlessness. Sabbath can be a powerful tool for resistance and recovery in this.

God is not glorified—and the culture is not renewed—when the church is filled with driven and exhausted Christians. In that light, practicing the Sabbath is not a burden but a gift that enables us to find rest, perspective, delight, and grace amid the pressures of a demanding culture.

This week the practice is to plan and celebrate a Sabbath and then share with one another what you learned about God, your life, and yourself.

BEFORE THE SESSION

Step 1: Individual Activity
Plan and practice a twenty-four-hour Sabbath this week, using the following four components.

Resist

What do I categorize as work? How can I build a barrier to resist it?

How can I resist the relentless intrusion of technology?

What boundaries can I put in place to make sure I am not interrupted?

How can I resist the temptation to turn my mind toward work?

Rest

How can I enjoy the following kinds of rest?
- spiritual rest
- physical rest
- emotional rest
- intellectual rest
- social rest

Remember

How do I acknowledge my limits as a created being?

How do I embrace my relationship with God?

How can I refocus on my identity in Christ?

How can I take the posture of John and delight in Jesus's heart?

Revel

What can I eat to the glory of God?

What can I watch, read, or do for the glory of God?

What brings me life, fills me with joy, and causes me to praise God?

What truth of Scripture can I delight in?

How can I fill my heart with beauty?

During the Session

Step 2: Group Discussion

1. How did your practice of the Sabbath go?

2. What was life giving about it? What was challenging about it?

3. What did it reveal to you about yourself and your current lifestyle?

4. What do you want to explore further about the practice of Sabbath?

5. Before reading this chapter, what was your understanding of the Sabbath?

6. From what you have learned and considered, what is the difference between a biblical Sabbath and simply taking a day off? Why is this distinction key?

7. Jon quoted Peter Scazzero's definition of the Sabbath: "The word *Sabbath* comes from the Hebrew word that means 'to cease, to stop working.' It refers to doing nothing related to work for a twenty-four hour period each week. It refers to this unit of time around which we are to orient our entire lives as 'holy,' meaning 'separate' . . . [from] the other six days. . . . Sabbath provides for us now an additional rhythm for an entire reorientation of our lives around the living God."[2] What stands out to you from this definition?

8. If you were to be really honest, is your current pace of life sustainable? Why, or why not?

9. What are the acute areas of pressure in your life?

10. Is the way you are currently living forming you into the image of Jesus or deforming you into the image of the world? How is this manifesting itself in your life?

11. Matitiahu Tsevat said that the biblical Sabbath means an "acceptance of the sovereignty of God."[3] How does Sabbath reveal submission to God?

12. In what ways does Sabbath strengthen discipleship?

13. How does Sabbath help you witness to those around you?

AFTER THE SESSION

Step 3: Reflection

As John Ortberg put it, "Again and again, as we pursue spiritual life, we must do battle with hurry. For many of us the great danger is not that we will renounce our faith. It is that we will become so distracted and rushed and preoccupied that we will settle for a mediocre version of it. We will just skim our lives instead of actually living them."[4]

Where are the battle zones in your war against hurry?

If you got rid of overbusyness in your life, what do you think would fill the space?

Session 4

Hunger Must Resist Apathy

In this chapter we explored our obsession with lesser desires that have numbed our spiritual senses, along with the power of fasting to cultivate hunger for God. As Bonhoeffer wrote in *The Cost of Discipleship,* "When the flesh is satisfied it is hard to pray with cheerfulness or to devote oneself to a life of service which calls for much self-renunciation."[5]

Fasting may be one of the most neglected practices of Christian discipleship in our day. Though fasting is talked about in our culture in regard to its health benefits (intermittent fasting, juice cleanses, etc.), it rarely seems as if it's a part of modern discipleship practice. But through both the Old and the New Testaments, fasting was seen as a regular and important part of life with God. It was a central practice in Jesus's own life and teaching.

Fasting pushes us to a fresh dependence on God, helps release spiritual burdens, and brings us to a place of repentance. Fasting also breaks through the spiritual apathy that lulls us to sleep in our cultural moment.

BEFORE THE SESSION

Step 1: Individual Activity

Do you need a breakthrough in some area of life or a deeper sense of intimacy with God? What do you sense God drawing you into? What has led to the need for this breakthrough? Why is this important to you?

Are you ready to conduct your own twenty-four-hour fast and to pray about this area?

Here are some steps to help you . . .

Starting the Fast

Mark off the time when you will fast and enter into conscious communion with God.

During the Fast

Tune your ear to the whisper of God. What impressions and insights are you gaining?

Be aware of the Enemy seeking to attack or tempt you. Satan launched his attack on Jesus when he was physically weak. What is the fast telling you about dependence, distraction, priorities, yourself, our culture?

Ending the Fast

Ease off the fast. The body can need some adjustment when it comes from a time of fasting. To signify the end of the time before God, give thanks to him for what you have experienced.

Examining the Fast

What happened in you?

What was revealed about your normal dependence? How did God speak to you?

What did you learn?

Share this with others in your community.

DURING THE SESSION

Step 2: Group Discussion

1. How did your practice of a twenty-four-hour fast go?

2. What was life giving about it? What was challenging about it?

3. What did it reveal to you about yourself, your current focus, and your dependence on food?

4. What is fasting, and how does it differ from dieting?

5. How does fasting dismantle apathy and awaken spiritual hunger? Did you experience this? Why, or why not?

6. Is there a part of you that resists or fears fasting? Name and examine any reasons fasting feels impossible.

7. How do fasting and prayer break through the secularity we see in our world today?

8. How can the concept of fasting affect other areas of our faith, such as self-control?

9. Do you think you will make fasting a regular part of your discipleship practice? Why, or why not?

10. In what ways can fasting become a life-giving, not legalistic, part of your walk with God?

After the Session

Step 3: Reflection

Jesus described apathetic Christians and compared them to a rejected meal.

> These are the words of the Amen, the faithful and true witness, the
> ruler of God's creation. I know your deeds, that you are neither cold nor
> hot. I wish you were either one or the other! So, because you are
> lukewarm—neither hot nor cold—I am about to spit you out of my
> mouth. (Revelation 3:14–16)

What did he want them to do? Recover their zeal and respond to his call.
If they did that, they could expect to feast with him.

> Be earnest and repent. Here I am! I stand at the door and knock. If
> anyone hears my voice and opens the door, I will come in and eat with
> that person, and they with me. (verses 19–20)

How could a lifestyle that involves fasting from food lead to spiritual feasting
for you?

Session 5

Hospitality Must Resist Fear

In this chapter we explored our tendency to fear the "other"—anyone outside our own familiar group or comfort zone. The media and polarization in the larger culture have caused us to dehumanize and demonize those different from us and fear them as threats to our lives and world. This happens in our political dialogue and in our own hearts and lives. Yet, in Philippians 2 and John 1, we see that Jesus descended to us and became like us, coming into our world and pitching his tent among us. Jesus then continually practiced hospitality by inviting other people into his life to eat with him, share with him, and even touch him. This week we want to move away from our culture's tendency to fear and avoid, and seek instead to become like Jesus—welcoming others into our lives and moving toward them with love and compassion.

BEFORE THE SESSION

Step 1: Individual Activity
Ask the Holy Spirit to guide you to someone who needs the hospitality and welcome of God in his (or her) life. Try to choose someone you would not naturally be drawn to—someone who represents crossing a boundary or whom it takes courage to move toward. (Obviously there is a need to be sensitive and wise in how you do this.)

Invite him out for a meal or coffee. Explain to him your desire to get to know others and break down the fear and hostility in our world.

Listen to his story without passing any sort of judgment or commenting. Ask questions about his background, perspective, current concerns, and situation.

Speak blessing, offer encouragement, and honor his story. Pay for his meal and thank him for his time.

Spend time afterward on your own, praying blessing over him and reflecting on what God revealed to you about your time together.

DURING THE SESSION

Step 2: Group Discussion

1. Whom did you eat a meal with or share coffee with to show hospitality this week?

2. Why did you choose that person? What happened?

3. What was life giving about the time together? What was challenging about it?

4. What did it reveal to you about yourself, your current friendships, and your understanding of those different from you?

5. Our culture's reaction to the other was described as a tendency to eliminate, assimilate, dominate, and demonize (page 82). Where have you seen this tendency at work in your community?

6. Is there any hint of this happening in your own heart? If you have the trust and courage, would you be willing to share?

7. *Hospitality* means "love of the stranger." How did Jesus model this?

8. Why is this so hard for us in our world today?

9. Jon highlighted this framework for the role hospitality plays in overcoming fear: *an environment of welcome + a transformation of identity = a new humanity.* What stands out to you about this framework?

10. What do you find challenging or hard about it in practice?

11. Why is opening our hearts and homes a good first step in deconstructing our fear?

12. How did the story of Derek Black and Matthew Stevenson inspire you? Is there anyone you sense God prompting you to reach out to in light of what you felt?

AFTER THE SESSION

Step 3: Reflection

Tim Chester said in his book *A Meal with Jesus,*

> There are three ways the New Testament completes the sentence, "The Son of Man came . . ." "The Son of Man came not to be served but to serve, and to give his life as a ransom for many . . . to seek and to save the lost . . . eating and drinking . . ." (Luke 7:34).
>
> The first two are statements of purpose. *Why* did Jesus come? He came to serve, to give his life as a ransom, to seek and save the lost. The third is a statement of method. *How* did Jesus come? He came eating and drinking.[6]

Spend some time thinking and praying about how a focus on hospitality can change your *mission* and *methods* in life. If you're married and perhaps have older children at home, discuss with them how you can establish new habits as a hospitable family.

$\mathfrak{Session}$ 6

Honor Must Resist Contempt

The Scriptures tell us to "outdo one another in showing honor" (Romans 12:10, ESV). What a foreign concept that is in our world so often driven by contempt!

Contempt is so dangerous for followers of Jesus because it creates a sense of superiority in us, devalues others, and also shuts off the work of God in our midst. Most of us would shudder at the thought that we show contempt to others, but it manifests itself in ways that we may not immediately recognize.

In this chapter, Jon discussed Arthur Brooks' description of hot hate versus cool hate. Brooks claims that hot hate is based on anger, while cool hate is based on contempt. Brooks said, "Cool hate can be every bit as damaging as hot hate. The social psychologist and relationship expert John Gottman was famously able to predict with up to 94 percent accuracy whether couples would divorce just by observing a brief snippet of conversation. The biggest warning signs of all were indications of contempt, such as sarcasm, sneering and hostile humor. . . . Disagreement is normal, but dismissiveness can be deadly."[7]

In this session we are going to look at how to overcome this deadly dismissiveness with the biblical value of honor. We will explore ways in which we can install honor, the operating system of heaven, in our lives, community, and culture.

BEFORE THE SESSION

Step 1: Individual Activity

Ask the Holy Spirit for guidance in identifying someone whom you can bestow honor on this week. Ask also for key words or insights that will be meaningful to that person.

Using the categories of the honor filter mentioned in this chapter, craft a letter to that person recognizing the value you see in her (or him). You may also want to meet with her and share in person what you have written.

Honor her *story*—moments from her journey that others may have overlooked. Recognize where she has come from and the details that make her life unique and important to you.

Honor her *calling*, whom God has made her to be and the kingdom vision you see in her. Call out the possibility in her life.

Honor her *sacrifice*. Try to think of smaller or more powerful moments that others may have overlooked, times she has gone the extra mile, put up with things, endured difficulty for the sake of living with integrity and following Jesus. (If she is not a believer, see whether you can honor the price she has paid to pursue her call or fulfill her responsibilities with integrity.)

Honor her *gifts*. What spiritual gifts, natural gifts, and developed gifts can you highlight and thank her for using? Is there a way these gifts have helped or blessed you? Be specific.

Remind her of her *future*. Where do you see God leading her? Where do you see her being in one, five, ten years? Remind her of key moments in her past, how you have seen God be faithful, and then speak into the future you believe God has for her.

There is such power in encouragement. Most people today hear feedback only when it's in the form of criticism. Honor can restore hope, overcome discouragement, and call people into their futures. Don't take this lightly; you never know what God may do.

DURING THE SESSION

Step 2: Group Discussion

1. Whom did you seek to honor this week?

2. Why did you choose that person?

2. What happened in your heart as you wrote that letter or met with that person?

3. What did it reveal to you about the power of honor and seeking to honor someone else?

4. Is there anyone else you sense the Spirit prompting you to honor this week?

5. Based on what you have learned about contempt this week, where do you most see it at work in your community?

6. Where do you most see contempt in the church?

7. Whom or what are you most likely to show contempt for?

8. Sometimes the contempt in our culture can bleed into the church. Jon mentioned several ways this can manifest itself. Contempt for God's power to do what he promised (seen in the children of Israel's failure to go into the promised land). Contempt for the work of the Spirit (grieving him or treating his gifts or ministry lightly). Contempt for Jesus's ministry (not believing he is who he says he is or becoming too familiar with him). Have you ever fallen prey to treating God in any of these ways? What happened to cause this?

9. How did you move away from this?

10. Of the five areas of the honor filter (honoring others' stories, callings, sacrifices, gifts, and futures), which is easiest for you to show to others? Which is hardest? Why?

Spend some time identifying anyone you may have shown contempt to and asking God to change your heart, and then pray a prayer of blessing over that person.

AFTER THE SESSION

Step 3: Reflection

Here are some of the places where the Scriptures mention honor. Spend some time meditating on and praying through these passages, and see whether God prompts you to reach out and honor someone in some way.

- *Honor is our destiny.* In Revelation 7:9–17, we learn that the nations will gather before the throne of God and honor the Lamb.
- *Honor is the relational framework of the Trinity.* In John 5:22–23, we are commanded to honor the Son as we honor the Father. The members of the Trinity relate to one another with honor.
- *All creation honors God.* In Isaiah 43:20–21, we read how even the wild animals honor God for his provision. If nature could talk, it would reveal its honor for the greatness of its Creator.
- *All human culture will honor God.* Isaiah 60:9 tells us that broken human culture will be redeemed and will recognize its place in the kingdom of God.
- *We are called to honor God with our sexuality.* First Corinthians 6:18–20 says that we belong to God and not ourselves and are to honor God with our bodies.
- *We are called to honor God with our wealth.* Proverbs 3:9–10 says that if we honor him first, we will be blessed and provided for. We are to honor God as the source of our provision.
- *We are called to honor God in our marriages.* First Peter 3:7 says that husbands should honor their wives or their prayers will be hindered. Marriage should be built on honor.

- *Honor is central in the home.* Ephesians 6:1–3 calls children to honor their parents—and promises blessing for doing so. Children are called to recognize the value and contribution of their parents in the home.
- *We are called to honor God in society.* Romans 13:1–7 states that we are to honor God-ordained authority. Honor makes cultural flourishing possible.
- *Honor should be the culture of the church.* First Timothy 5:17 states that leaders who do their job well are worthy of double honor, the only place in the Scriptures where double honor is mentioned. Honoring leaders should define the Christian congregation.
- *We are called to honor one another.* Romans 12:10 tells us that we should "outdo one another in showing honor" (ESV). It should be a distinctive of how the people of God treat one another.

Session 7

Love Must Resist Hate

In this session we explored the deep and challenging topic of love resisting hate. Words like these are easy to say but incredibly hard to live out. Loving our enemies is the distinctive mark of a follower of Jesus. It is distinctive because it is impossible without him. Enemy love is supernatural work that only God can do in our hearts. Saint Augustine wrote, "Many have learned how to offer the other cheek, but do not know how to love him by whom they are struck."[8]

BEFORE THE SESSION

Step 1: Individual Activity

All love for our enemies is rooted in our ability to forgive them. Ask the Holy Spirit to search your heart and reveal any bitterness harbored in your heart. With a posture of openness and asking the Spirit for his help, follow the five Rs of forgiveness.

Recognize

Make a list of the ways in which a person has offended you. Be honest and specific but not petty. Don't skim over the conflict or resistance you feel.

Remember

Check the motives of your heart. Is there any pride, bitterness, desire for revenge? Hand things over to God, and invite him into these places in your heart.

Spend some time meditating on the Cross and your own sin and brokenness. In what ways has God shown you mercy? For what has he forgiven you?

Remember the backstory of the other person, not just the offense. What has that person gone through that may have contributed to his (or her) treatment of you?

Release

Release the person from his (or her) debt. Consciously forgive him, and announce that verdict over him in your heart. Ask God to give you strength to love the person and see him as God does.

You may want to use the script below as a starting point.

Father, forgive me for holding unforgiveness against [add name]. Give me your strength to forgive, and enable me to release this person from the unforgiveness in my heart. I forgive him [or her]. In Jesus's name, amen.

Resolve

Resolve to "make every effort to keep the unity of the Spirit through the bond of peace" (Ephesians 4:3).

Resolve to leave the hurt in the past and not bring it up or hold it over the person.

How can you *show love* to this person?

How can you *do good* to this person?

How can you *bless* this person?

How can you *pray* for this person?

Rejoice

Celebrate the healing power of the Cross. Rejoice in this breakthrough and step of progress toward enemy love. Though this may seem small, this is how cycles of hate and bitterness and violence end. Someone breaks the flow of hate.

Rejoice that the burden of hate has been taken off your life. Rejoice in the reality that your character is becoming more like Christ's.

DURING THE SESSION

Step 2: Group Discussion

1. Enemy love can be hard. Forgiving those who have deeply hurt us can be both painful and a process of God's grace. This week our practice of forgiveness was a first step toward enemy love. What did the thought of this practice stir up in your heart?

2. What was hard about this? What was freeing about this?

3. Are there any next steps you sense God may be asking you to take in regard to your relationship to this person?

4. Who is the first person in your childhood whom you would describe as your enemy? How did that conflict shape your perspective in the rest of your life?

5. Jon mentioned the scene in *1984* (Two Minutes Hate) where the citizens scream and release their anger toward their perceived enemy

(pages 114–16). In what way do you see the media cultivating anger and hate in your heart? Would you be willing to share an example?

6. The story of Dr. King protecting and hugging his white supremacist attacker is a prophetic picture of how we are called to love our enemies (pages 122–23). Have you ever encountered a situation like this or responded in a similar manner? Who was your enemy, and what happened?

7. In what way does this show us a picture of the Cross?

8. Enemy love was a defining mark of the Christian church for the first three hundred years. What forces do you see at work that have changed our messaging today?

9. In what way does the story of the car accident and subsequent forgiveness (pages 123–24) inspire you to show small acts of enemy love in our conflict-ridden world today?

Spend some time praying as a group for those in your community who are considered enemies. Then brainstorm some tangible ways you can bless them and do good this week.

AFTER THE SESSION

Step 3: Reflection

Read and meditate on the following verses. What stands out to you? Why? What do you sense God prompting you to do?

> You have heard that it was said, "Love your neighbor and hate your enemy." But I tell you, love your enemies and pray for those who persecute you, that you may be children of your Father in heaven. He causes his sun to rise on the evil and the good, and sends rain on the righteous and the unrighteous. If you love those who love you, what reward will you get? Are not even the tax collectors doing that? And if you greet only your own people, what are you doing more than others? Do not even pagans do that? Be perfect, therefore, as your heavenly Father is perfect. (Matthew 5:43–48)

These verses are not just *part* of our faith but *central* to our faith. As Preston Sprinkle wrote,

> Jesus's command to "love your enemies" was the most popular verse in the early church. It was quoted in 26 places by 10 different writers in the first 300 years of Christianity, which makes it *the* most celebrated command among the first Christians. Matthew 5:44 was the so-called John 3:16 of the early church. And enemy-love was the hallmark of the Christian faith. Other religions taught that people should love their neighbors. They even taught forgiveness for those who wronged them. But actually *loving your enemy*? Only Jesus and his followers took love this far. Because this is how far the love of God extends to us—"while we were God's *enemies*" Christ loved us.[9]

Sacrifice Must Resist Privilege

Chapter 8 looks at a heavily contested idea in our culture—that of privilege. Though the concept of privilege can be controversial, almost all of us would acknowledge that we have some level of inherited cultural advantage that we didn't earn. What do we do with that as followers of Jesus? Should we accept that reality and enjoy it or feel guilty and paralyzed by shame? The answer is neither response.

We are called to resist the selfish enjoyment of privilege by redirecting it in sacrificial service of others. This is the posture that the world is aching for the church to take and that God looks for in those who claim to be followers of his Son. It's this voluntary redirection when not culturally required that shows the love of God to the world. As Andy Crouch has said, "The most transformative acts of our lives are likely to be the moments when we radically empty ourselves, in the very settings where we would normally be expected to exercise authority."[10]

BEFORE THE SESSION

Step 1: Individual Activity

Identify someone in your life or in close proximity who has less privilege than you do. (Ask the Holy Spirit to reveal the right person so you don't immediately jump to stereotyping or responding in a messianic way.) Identify some way you can bless or serve that person in secret. Try to make this as meaningful and empowering as possible. This is best done in secret to break any sort of power dynamic or unintended condescension.

Whom do you feel led to sacrificially serve?

What are you going to do to serve and empower that person?

In what way is this a meaningful sacrifice for you?

I am aware that small gestures like this may appear somewhat inconsequential in light of the brokenness and need of the world. But we must start somewhere. Small practices with great intentionality can reform our instincts and habits and lead to larger changes in our lives over time.

I am reminded of a friend of mine who studied for years and eventually earned his PhD with the goal of becoming a tenured professor. After teaching for years, he finally came up for consideration for tenure. Another professor, a minority woman, was also being considered. The first to earn a doctorate in her family, she was remarkably gifted, and he knew she would do a good job. So he recommended her for his own position. He did this with joy, even though it involved real sacrifice of his academic ambitions.

His response deeply affected me: "I am a white man with advanced degrees from some of the best schools in the world. I will have doors open for me with some level of ease and be fine. But for this gifted woman who will do an incredible job, this could change the family dynamic and empower those who come behind in real ways. As a follower of Jesus, it's a joy to get to be a part of this."

How does someone learn that instinct? He had been cultivating a life of sacrifice in small and meaningful ways for years, and his theology of love and empowerment had prepared him for this moment over time.

During the Session

Step 2: Group Discussion

1. Jon opened the chapter with a story about the first time he realized he was experiencing privilege. He was taken to the front of the line at the INS because he was from Australia (pages 129–30). Have you ever had

a moment of recognizing your privilege like this? What happened? How did it make you feel?

2. In this chapter *privilege* was defined as "unearned access to resources (social power) that are only readily available to some people because of their social group membership; an advantage, or immunity granted to or enjoyed by one societal group above and beyond the common advantage of all other groups."[11] What stands out to you in this definition? Do you agree or disagree with it? Why, or why not?

3. Where do you see the reality of privilege in your community today?

4. Jon mentioned there are normally two responses in our discussions of privilege: defensiveness ("I don't have privilege; I have earned everything I have") and responsibility ("Get your own life together and stop being a victim"). How have you seen these responses in your own heart? In what ways are they incompatible with what we see in the life of Jesus?

5. Jon mentioned game theory and the gospel (pages 137–38): (1) *I win; you lose,* (2) *Win-win,* and (3) *I sacrifice; you win.* Why is *I win; you lose* incompatible with the gospel as a paradigm for life?

6. In what ways is *win-win* a surface response to the gospel?

7. In what ways is *I sacrifice; you win* manifest in the life of Jesus?

8. What would it take to embrace this framework in your life?

9. Extending the borders of our hearts is one of the key ideas related to caring for those with less privilege. In what practical ways can you enlarge your heart to care about more people?

10. In what ways can you redirect privilege in the following areas?
    • your time and margin
    • your education and learning
    • your finances
    • your physical assets, home, vacation home
    • your mobility

Spend some time praying that God will sort entitlement out of your heart and replace it with compassion, servanthood, and a willingness to sacrifice.

AFTER THE SESSION

Step 3: Reflection

Meditate on and pray through Philippians 2:1–11:

> If you have any encouragement from being united with Christ, if any
> comfort from his love, if any common sharing in the Spirit, if any
> tenderness and compassion, then make my joy complete by being
> like-minded, having the same love, being one in spirit and of one mind.
> Do nothing out of selfish ambition or vain conceit. Rather, in humility
> value others above yourselves, not looking to your own interests but
> each of you to the interests of the others.
>
> In your relationships with one another, have the same mindset as
> Christ Jesus:
>
> Who, being in very nature God,
>   did not consider equality with God something to be used to his
>   own advantage;
> rather, he made himself nothing
>   by taking the very nature of a servant,
>   being made in human likeness.
> And being found in appearance as a man,
>   he humbled himself
>   by becoming obedient to death—
>   even death on a cross!

What words or phrases stand out to you?

What in this passage is most challenging to you?

What people come to mind when you think about the implications of these verses?

How does this passage stir love for Jesus in you?

How is God prompting you to sacrificially serve those around you?

How will you take a step toward sacrificial service this week?

Session 9

Celebration Must Resist Cynicism / Epilogue

When you think of the following events, what comes to mind?

- the Carnival in Brazil
- Mardi Gras in New Orleans
- Oktoberfest in Munich, Germany
- the Carnival of Venice, Italy

Now, what is the first thing that comes to mind when you hear the following words?

- God
- Jesus
- church
- Christianity

Christians have somehow developed a reputation as angry, bitter, and judgmental people who rob our world of joy and celebration, rather than as people who bring and define celebration. Not only is the church seen as being anti-celebration, but our church culture also often flattens moments of significance, wonder, and gratitude in favor of efficiency. We rarely even seem to notice the beauty and glory of the work of God in the world around us—or even in our own lives. Why aren't we known for what Jesus promised us—joy?

Celebration, then, is not a secondary issue but a central one, if we are to represent Jesus well in our world today. We need to embrace Jesus's radically generous, unreasonable, scandalous joy in our lives. We need to mark our moments with holy wonder. This enables us to resist temptation, delight in God, and invite the world to embrace the good news we share. As John Ortberg wrote, "We must arrange life so that sin no longer looks good to us."[12]

BEFORE THE SESSION

Step 1: Individual Activity

In the Old Testament, the children of God were given a redemptive calendar to celebrate major events and the work of God in their midst. This became a way of building their lives around the activity of God and not just the pressures and demands around them.

In that tradition, we all have our own stories of redemption. We all have sacred moments of God's work in our lives that we should memorialize and celebrate.

Draw a time line of your life across a sheet of paper, and then take time to think through the ways God has been kind and faithful to you. Name these key events, and write the dates they happened.

What made these events so meaningful?

How were you aware of God at work in these events?

What did they reveal to you about God's character?

How did they shape your story?

Why are they worthy of celebration?

DURING THE SESSION

Step 2: Group Discussion

Start the time by having a couple of people share their redemptive calendars.

1. What can you celebrate along with the others in the group? How does this inspire joy in you?

2. What barriers to joy are in your life?

3. Where do you find cynicism leaking into your heart? Why is this toxic for followers of Jesus?

4. Of the things mentioned in this chapter that are framed by celebration (creation, tithing, Scripture, jubilee), which one was most surprising to you? Which one made you rethink your approach to it?

5. Jon mentioned on pages 155–56 that we have a joy center in our brains and it's possible for it to override some of our base instincts. What specific practices do you think would strengthen your own joy center?

6. How can you as a community begin to bring more celebration to your life together? Spend a few moments thinking through and discussing some ways to build this into your rhythm.

7. As you think back over the topics covered in *Beautiful Resistance,* what is the area where you most feel called by God to offer resistance to the un-Christlike trends in society? Why that one?

8. Jon said, "How would things change if you resolved to rebel against your own indifference and embody the things you long to see in the world? If you resolved that you would pursue beauty and resist brokenness? That you would resist idolatry with worship, exhaustion with rest, apathy with hunger, fear with hospitality, contempt with honor, hate with love, privilege with sacrifice, and cynicism with celebration? If your life became a parable of what happens when someone lives with integrity

and in community no matter the cost?" What kinds of impact do you think you could have in the world if you became more intentional about choosing the gospel and biblical values over the easy way offered by culture?

Spend some time praying for one another.

AFTER THE SESSION

Step 3: Reflection

This week, try to spend one day noticing and enjoying all the good gifts you've been given and the things you love about life. As Richard Foster said, "God's normal means of bringing his joy is by redeeming and sanctifying the ordinary junctures of human life."[13]

What small things do you enjoy? Infuse those with celebration.

- drinking a flat white while sitting in the sun
- strolling through a park with hints of changing foliage
- listening to a favorite song
- rereading something you have cherished over the years
- experiencing a small victory in your walk with God
- playing your favorite sport with friends

Try to elevate this experience above the normal flow of life.

A new movement of resistance can start with small steps taken in joy.

ACKNOWLEDGMENTS

Like all things that really matter, this book had a team of people, often unseen, who worked without credit to make it possible. I want to acknowledge the support and help of many who believed a beautiful resistance is worth fighting for. I am profoundly grateful for you.

My extraordinary wife, Christy, you model defiant joy in the midst of so much resistance.

My children, Nathan and Haley, the joy and pride in my heart are in you. Thanks for being willing to sleep in a microcar in Poland to find Finkenwalde.

Andrew Stoddard, you've believed in me and supported me and have been a remarkably kind and generous man. This would not be possible without you.

Eric Stanford, this book is so much better because of your work. Thanks for adding so much value.

Shawn Smucker, thanks for helping me break the back on a few tough chapters.

Jonah Langenderfer, thanks for your thoughtful and faithful help in research. I am truly grateful.

Joe Beery, thanks for digging deep for obscure sources and fresh insights. Connective tissue for days.

Church of the City New York, thanks for living out so much of what is written here. You make pastoring a joy.

The Bon Hill Community, you left me alone for the summer and didn't judge me so I could finish the manuscript.

I am also deeply grateful for my brothers and sisters in the persecuted church around the world. I think and pray for you often. You embody what I only aspire to. Grace and peace.

NOTES

Introduction

1. H. Gaylon Barker, "Editor's Introduction to the English Edition," in Dietrich Bonhoeffer, *Theological Education at Finkenwalde: 1935–1937*, ed. H. Gaylon Barker and Mark Brocker, trans. Douglas W. Stott, vol. 14 of *Dietrich Bonhoeffer Works*, ed. Victoria J. Barnett and Barbara Wojhoski (Minneapolis: Augsburg Fortress, 2013), 5.
2. Dietrich Bonhoeffer, *Life Together*, in *Life Together and Prayerbook of the Bible*, ed. Geffrey B. Kelly, Gerhard Ludwig Müller, and Albrecht Schönherr, trans. Daniel W. Bloesch and James H. Burtness, vol. 5 of *Dietrich Bonhoeffer Works*, ed. Wayne Whitson Floyd Jr. (Minneapolis: Fortress, 2005), 29.
3. Wilhelm Niesel, "From Keelson to Principal of a Seminary," in *I Knew Dietrich Bonhoeffer*, ed. Wolf-Dieter Zimmermann and Ronald Gregor Smith, trans. Käthe Gregor Smith (New York: Harper & Row, 1966), 146.
4. Charles Marsh, *Strange Glory: A Life of Dietrich Bonhoeffer* (New York: Vintage Books, 2014), 256–57. Marsh quoted Niesel from "From Keelson to Principal," 146.
5. See the research of the Pinetops Foundation and its work on the state of the church at greatopportunity.org.

Chapter 1: A Church Coming Back to Life

1. Seth Stephens-Davidowitz, "Googling for God," *New York Times*, September 19, 2015, www.nytimes.com/2015/09/20/opinion/sunday/seth-stephens-davidowitz-googling-for-god.html.

2. Friedrich Nietzsche, *Thus Spake Zarathustra: A Book for Everyone and Nobody*, trans. Graham Parkes (Oxford: Oxford University Press, 2005), 79.

3. Frank Viola, *From Eternity to Here: Rediscovering the Ageless Purpose of God* (Colorado Springs, CO: David C Cook, 2009), 25.

4. Rob Bell, *Sex God: Exploring the Endless Connections Between Sexuality and Spirituality* (Grand Rapids, MI: Zondervan, 2007), 131–32.

5. Viola, *From Eternity to Here*, 62–63.

6. See 2 Corinthians 6:16 and its reference to Old Testament promises about God dwelling among his people.

7. Quoted in G. K. Beale and Mitchell Kim, *God Dwells Among Us: Expanding Eden to the Ends of the Earth* (Downers Grove, IL: InterVarsity, 2014), 99.

8. Philip Yancey, *Prayer: Does It Make Any Difference?* (Grand Rapids, MI: Zondervan, 2006), 273–74.

9. Yancey, *Prayer*, 274.

10. C. S. Lewis, "The Efficacy of Prayer," in *"The World's Last Night" and Other Essays* (1952; repr., Orlando, FL: Harcourt, 2002), 9.

11. Viola, *From Eternity to Here*, 236–37.

12. Jean-Dominique Bauby, *The Diving Bell and the Butterfly*, trans. Jeremy Leggatt (New York: Knopf, 1997), 77.

Chapter 2: Worship Must Resist Idolatry

1. Bruce Ellis Benson, *Graven Ideologies: Nietzsche, Derrida & Marion on Modern Idolatry* (Downers Grove, IL: InterVarsity, 2002), 19.

2. William Stringfellow, *Imposters of God: Inquiries into Favorite Idols* (Eugene, OR: Wipf & Stock, 2006), 5–6.

3. "Answer 105," in Westminster Larger Catechism, July 2, 1648, www .apuritansmind.com/westminster-standards/larger-catechism.

4. Timothy Keller, *Counterfeit Gods: The Empty Promises of Money, Sex, and Power, and the Only Hope That Matters* (New York: Riverhead Books, 2011), xix.

5. Elyse M. Fitzpatrick, *Idols of the Heart: Learning to Long for God Alone*, 2nd ed. (Phillipsburg, NJ: P&R, 2016), 28.

6. David K. Naugle, *Reordered Love, Reordered Lives: Learning the Deep Meaning of Happiness* (Grand Rapids, MI: Eerdmans, 2008), 49–50.

7. David Powlison, "Idols of the Heart and 'Vanity Fair,'" *Journal of Biblical Counseling* 13, no. 2 (Winter 1995): 36.

8. Mary Douglas, *Natural Symbols: Explorations in Cosmology* (1970; repr., New York: Routledge, 2002).

9. Peter Berger, *The Sacred Canopy: Elements of a Sociological Theory of Religion* (Garden City, NY: Doubleday, 1967), 45.

10. David Foster Wallace, *This Is Water: Some Thoughts, Delivered on a Significant Occasion, About Living a Compassionate Life* (New York: Little, Brown, 2009), 102–10.

11. George Packer, "Ten Years After the Crash," *New Yorker*, August 19, 2018, www.newyorker.com/magazine/2018/08/27/ten-years-after -the-crash.

12. Philip Yancey, *Church: Why Bother? My Personal Pilgrimage* (Grand Rapids, MI: Zondervan, 1998), 25.

13. James K. A. Smith, *Who's Afraid of Postmodernism? Taking Derrida, Lyotard, and Foucault to Church* (Grand Rapids, MI: Baker Academic, 2006), 107.

14. "What really needs to be said is that where the Church is faithful to its Lord, there the powers of the kingdom are present and people begin to ask the question to which the gospel is the answer." Lesslie Newbigin, *The Gospel in a Pluralist Society* (Grand Rapids, MI: Eerdmans, 1989), 119.

Chapter 3: Rest Must Resist Exhaustion

1. Dorothy Victor, "Are We There Yet?," *Deccan Herald,* September 27, 2015, www.deccanherald.com/content/503003/are-we-yet.html; Mitchell R. Haney, "The Value of Slow," in *The Value of Time and Leisure in a World of Work,* ed. Mitchell R. Haney and A. David Kline (Lanham, MD: Lexington Books, 2010), 152–53.

2. Derek Thompson, "Workism Is Making Americans Miserable," *Atlantic,* February 24, 2019, www.theatlantic.com/ideas/archive/2019/02/religion -workism-making-americans-miserable/583441.

3. Samuel P. Huntington, quoted in Thompson, "Workism."

4. Sheldon Cohen, Denise Janicki-Deverts, and Gregory E. Miller, "Psycho- logical Stress and Disease," *Journal of the American Medical Association* 298, no. 14 (2007): 1685–87. Quoted in Haney, "The Value of Slow," in *Value of Time and Leisure,* 154.

5. Carl Honoré, *In Praise of Slowness: Challenging the Cult of Speed* (San Francisco: HarperSanFrancisco, 2005), 2.

6. Thomas Merton, *Conjectures of a Guilty Bystander* (New York: Image Books, 2009), 81.

7. A. J. Swoboda, *Subversive Sabbath: The Surprising Power of Rest in a Nonstop World* (Grand Rapids, MI: Brazos, 2018), 5. Quote rearranged.

8. Peter Scazzero, *Emotionally Healthy Spirituality: It's Impossible to Be Spiritually Mature While Remaining Emotionally Immature,* rev. ed. (Grand Rapids, MI: Zondervan, 2017), 150.

9. Larry Dossey, quoted in Honoré, *In Praise of Slowness,* 3.

10. Honoré, *In Praise of Slowness,* 4, 33.

11. Abraham Joshua Heschel, *The Sabbath: Its Meaning for Modern Man* (1951; repr., New York: Farrar, Straus and Giroux, 2005), 98–99.

12. These four movements are inspired by Marva J. Dawn, *Keeping the Sabbath Wholly: Ceasing, Resting, Embracing, Feasting* (1989; repr., Grand Rapids, MI: Eerdmans, 2002).

13. Dawn, *Keeping the Sabbath Wholly,* 76.

14. Matitiahu Tsevat, quoted in Dawn, *Keeping the Sabbath Wholly,* 57.

15. Dawn, *Keeping the Sabbath Wholly,* 69.

16. William L. Holladay, ed., *A Concise Hebrew and Aramaic Lexicon of the Old Testament* (Leiden, Netherlands: Brill, 2000), 242. There is a lot of discussion about this word. Is it simply an anthropomorphism, or does it describe a kind of pleasure God took in reflecting on the creation of the world? My goal here is not to parse the technicalities of this word but to sit in the wonder of the restorative power of Sabbath.

17. Al Gini, "The Effects of Work on Moral Decision-Making," in *Value of Time and Leisure,* 141.

18. Thompson, "Workism."

19. Swoboda, *Subversive Sabbath,* 17.

20. John Ortberg, *The Life You've Always Wanted: Spiritual Disciplines for Ordinary People* (Grand Rapids, MI: Zondervan, 2002), 66.

21. Philo, *On the Account of the World's Creation Given by Moses,* trans. F. H. Colson and G. H. Whitaker, vol. 1 of *Philo: In Ten Volumes* (Cambridge, MA: Harvard University Press, 1981), 73.

22. Swoboda, *Subversive Sabbath,* xii.

Chapter 4: Hunger Must Resist Apathy

1. C. S. Lewis, "The Weight of Glory," in *The Weight of Glory: And Other Addresses,* rev. ed. (New York: HarperOne, 2001), 31.

2. Ruby K. Payne, *A Framework for Understanding Poverty: A Cognitive Approach,* 5th ed. (Highlands, TX: aha! Process, 2013), 54–55.

3. Richard J. Foster, *Celebration of Discipline: The Path to Spiritual Growth,* 2nd ed. (New York: Harper & Row, 1988), 55.

4. John Piper, *A Hunger for God: Desiring God Through Fasting and Prayer* (Wheaton, IL: Crossway, 2013), 18. Quote rearranged.

5. Jentezen Franklin, *Fasting: Opening the Door to a Deeper, More Intimate, More Powerful Relationship with God* (Lake Mary, FL: Charisma House, 2011), 35–36.

6. Much pastoral wisdom is required here. Because of our culture's obsessive and unhealthy emphasis on food and body image, many people have struggled with their sense of worth and body image. I certainly would not like to suggest something that would further complicate this reality or create a form of Christian legalism. Jesus is so patient and kind with us and accepts all genuine acts of worship and discipline.

7. The term *King Stomach* is used by Jentezen Franklin in his short but solid book entitled *Fasting*.

8. C. S. Lewis, *The Lion, the Witch and the Wardrobe* (1950; repr., London: HarperCollins Children's Books, 2015), 36–38.

9. Dan B. Allender, *To Be Told: God Invites You to Coauthor Your Future* (Colorado Springs, CO: WaterBrook, 2005), 186.

10. Franklin, *Fasting,* 72–73.

11. Josh M. Shepherd, "How a Confederate Memorial Became a Multiracial Worship Site," *Christianity Today,* September 7, 2018, www .christianitytoday.com/news/2018/september/stone-mountain -confederate-onerace-atlanta.html. This whole article is worth reading and presents a powerful blueprint for what God could do in cities across America.

12. Elie Wiesel, *Night,* trans. Marion Wiesel (New York: Hill and Wang, 2006), 69.

Chapter 5: Hospitality Must Resist Fear

1. See Eli Saslow, "The White Flight of Derek Black," *Washington Post,* October 15, 2016, www.washingtonpost.com/national/the-white-flight -of-derek-black/2016/10/15/ed5f906a-8f3b-11e6-a6a3-d50061aa9fae _story.html?utm_term=.c7ede592a459; "Don Black/Stormfront," Anti-Defamation League, 2012, www.adl.org/sites/default/files /documents/assets/pdf/combating-hate/Don-Black.pdf.

2. Georg Wilhelm Friedrich Hegel, *Lectures on the Philosophy of Religion: The Lectures of 1827,* ed. Peter C. Hodgson, trans. R. F. Brown, P. C.

Hodgson, and J. M. Stewart (Berkeley: University of California Press, 1988), 418. His definition is somewhat complex and is almost unrecognizable compared with how the term is used in modern sociology: "This other . . . has its self-consciousness only in me, and both the other and I are only this consciousness of being-outside-ourselves and of our identity; we are only this intuition, feeling, and knowledge of our unity. This is love, and without knowing that love is both a distinguishing and the sublation of the distinction, one speaks emptily of it."

3. Mina Cikara, quoted in Brian Resnick, "What Brexit Can Teach Us About the Psychology of Fear," Vox, June 25, 2016, www.vox.com /2016/6/25/12023768/brexit-psychology-fear.

4. Miroslav Volf, *Exclusion & Embrace: A Theological Exploration of Identity, Otherness, and Reconciliation* (Nashville: Abingdon, 1996), 60.

5. Andrew Shepherd, *The Gift of the Other: Levinas, Derrida, and a Theology of Hospitality* (Cambridge, UK: Clarke, 2014), 246.

6. Shepherd, *The Gift of the Other*, 4–9.

7. Christine D. Pohl, *Making Room: Recovering Hospitality as a Christian Tradition* (Grand Rapids, MI: Eerdmans, 1999), 7–8.

8. Joshua W. Jipp, *Saved by Faith and Hospitality* (Grand Rapids, MI: Eerdmans, 2017), 22.

9. Jipp, *Saved by Faith and Hospitality*, 17.

10. Tim Chester, *A Meal with Jesus: Discovering Grace, Community, and Mission Around the Table* (Wheaton, IL: Crossway, 2011), 13, quoting Robert J. Karris, *Eating Your Way Through Luke's Gospel* (Collegeville, MN: Liturgical Press, 2006), 14.

11. Jacques Derrida, "Foreigner Question," in *Of Hospitality: Anne Dufourmantelle Invites Jacques Derrida to Respond*, trans. Rachel Bowlby (Stanford, CA: Stanford University Press, 2000), 25.

12. Jipp, *Saved by Faith and Hospitality*, 2.

13. I heard him say this in a fellows cohort around 2008.

14. The city was unfortunately a little less excited than I was. Dan Piepen-bring, "Chick-fil-A's Creepy Infiltration of New York," *New Yorker,* April 13, 2018, www.newyorker.com/culture/annals-of-gastronomy/chick-fil-as-creepy-infiltration-of-new-york-city.

15. Alan Hirsch and Lance Ford, *Right Here, Right Now: Everyday Mission for Everyday People* (Grand Rapids, MI: Baker Books, 2011), 51.

16. Skye Jethani, *The Divine Commodity: Discovering a Faith Beyond Consumer Christianity* (Grand Rapids, MI: Zondervan, 2009), 153–54.

17. Krish Kandiah, *God Is Stranger: Finding God in Unexpected Places* (Downers Grove, IL: IVP Books, 2017), 12.

18. Bob Ekblad, quoted in Kandiah, *God Is Stranger,* 282.

19. Quoted in Saslow, "White Flight."

20. Quoted in Charlayne Hunter-Gault, "Derek Black Grew Up As a White Nationalist. Here's How He Changed His Mind," *PBS NewsHour,* November 5, 2019, www.pbs.org/newshour/show/derek-black-grew-up-as-a-white-nationalist-heres-how-he-changed-his-mind.

21. Saslow, "White Flight."

22. Derek Black, "Leaving White Nationalism," *Intelligence Report,* August 21, 2013, www.splcenter.org/fighting-hate/intelligence-report/2013/leaving-white-nationalism.

23. Henri J. M. Nouwen, *Reaching Out: The Three Movements of the Spiritual Life* (New York: Image Books, 1986), 65–66.

Chapter 6: Honor Must Resist Contempt

1. Publilius Syrus, *The Moral Sayings of Publius Syrus, a Roman Slave,* trans. Darius Lyman (Cleveland: Barnard, 1856), 31.

2. Arthur C. Brooks, "The Thrill of Political Hating," *New York Times,* June 8, 2015, www.nytimes.com/2015/06/08/opinion/the-thrill-of-political-hating.html.

3. Sebastian Junger, *Tribe: On Homecoming and Belonging* (New York: Twelve, 2016), 125–26.

4. William Ian Miller, *The Anatomy of Disgust* (Cambridge, MA: Harvard University Press, 1997), 214.

5. Robert C. Solomon, "The Emotional Register: Who's Who Among the Passions," chap. 8 in *The Passions: Emotions and the Meaning of Life* (Indianapolis: Hackett, 1993).

6. Ben Sasse, *Them: Why We Hate Each Other—and How to Heal* (New York: St. Martin's, 2018), 103.

7. Oli H. Anderson, *Synchronesia: A Depressing Existential Novel* (Scotts Valley, CA: CreateSpace, 2015), 195.

8. Various ethnographies have described cultures of honor in great detail. Sociologist Elijah Anderson, for example, has written about the culture of honor in inner cities of the United States. Anthropologists Julian Pitt-Rivers and J. G. Peristiany have written about honor in the Mediterranean region, and an important collection of papers can be found in Peristiany's 1966 book *Honour and Shame: The Values of Mediterranean Society*. Notably, the book includes chapters by Pitt-Rivers, Peristiany, and Pierre Bourdieu, who has written about honor and the importance of female chastity among the Kabyle of Algeria. As in many Mediterranean cultures, the sanctity of the family name among the Kabyle depends a great deal on the purity of its women and how well the men guard and protect it. In such cultures, females who disgrace the family may be killed by their male relatives in an attempt to cleanse the family name. I am referring not to this traditional sort of honor culture (purity honor) but to civil honor—the implicit recognition of the humanity and value of others.

9. "5091. Timaó," Bible Hub, https://biblehub.com/greek/5091.htm.

10. Joseph L. Umidi, *Transformational Intelligence: Creating Cultures of Honor @ Home and Work* (Virginia Beach, VA: Lifeforming Institute, 2014), 12.

11. C. S. Lewis, *The Problem of Pain* (1940; repr., New York: HarperOne, 2001), 46.

12. Stephen R. Covey, *The 7 Habits of Highly Effective People: Powerful Lessons in Personal Change*, 25th anniv. ed. (New York: Simon & Schuster, 2013), 38–39.

13. Umidi, *Transformational Intelligence*, 13.

14. Umidi, *Transformational Intelligence*, 16.

15. Philip Yancey, *Rumors of Another World: What on Earth Are We Missing?* (Grand Rapids, MI: Zondervan, 2003), 197–98.

Chapter 7: Love Must Resist Hate

1. Michael Ignatieff, "The Way We Live Now: 09-09-01: Exhibit A; Blood Sisters," *New York Times*, September 9, 2001, www.nytimes.com/2001 /09/09/magazine/the-way-we-live-now-09-09-01-exhibit-a-blood-sisters .html; see Stephen Castle, "Nuns Convicted of Mass Slaughter in Rwandan Convent," *Independent*, June 9, 2001, www.independent .co.uk/news/world/africa/nuns-convicted-of-mass-slaughter-in-rwandan -convent-9227307.html.

2. George Orwell, *1984* (1949; repr., New York: New American Library, 2019), 14.

3. Watch "Two Minutes Hate" on YouTube and see whether you can see any modern parallels: www.youtube.com/watch?v=t4zYlOU7Fpk.

4. Dylann Roof, quoted in Tonya Maxwell, "Convicted Killer Dylann Roof: 'I Am Not Sorry,'" *USA Today*, January 5, 2017, www.usatoday .com/story/news/nation-now/2017/01/05/dylann-roof-statements /96197870.

5. Preston Sprinkle, "Love Your . . . Enemies? Grace, Nonviolence, Pacifism," PrestonSprinkle.com, August 31, 2016, www.prestonsprinkle .com/blog/2016/8/31/love-yourenemies.

6. This story is adapted from Malcolm Gladwell, *David and Goliath: Underdogs, Misfits, and the Art of Battling Giants* (New York: Little, Brown, 2013), 175.

7. Paul Moses, *The Saint and the Sultan: The Crusades, Islam and Francis of Assisi's Mission of Peace* (New York: Doubleday Religion, 2009), 107–46. From my perspective, this is one of the most important accounts of the Crusades because it provides a picture of integrity and hope in the midst of one of the greatest stains in the history of the church.

8. Quoted in Mark Berman, "'I Forgive You.' Relatives of Charleston Church Shooting Victims Address Dylann Roof," *Washington Post*, June 19, 2015, www.washingtonpost.com/news/post-nation/wp/2015 /06/19/i-forgive-you-relatives-of-charleston-church-victims-address -dylann-roof/?utm_term=.27b6994b42ef.

Chapter 8: Sacrifice Must Resist Privilege

1. "What Is Privilege?," National Conference for Community and Justice, https://nccj.org/what-privilege.

2. Sian Ferguson, "Privilege 101: A Quick and Dirty Guide," Everyday Feminism, September 29, 2014, https://everydayfeminism.com/2014 /09/what-is-privilege.

3. Daysha Edewi, "What Is Privilege?," BuzzFeed, July 4, 2015, www .buzzfeed.com/dayshavedewi/what-is-privilege. Paraphrased.

4. Kimberlé Crenshaw, "Demarginalizing the Intersection of Race and Sex: A Black Feminist Critique of Antidiscrimination Doctrine, Feminist Theory and Antiracist Politics," *University of Chicago Legal Forum* 1989, no. 1 (1989): 149, https://chicagounbound.uchicago.edu/uclf/vol1989 /iss1/8.

5. This story ended well. The church came around him and helped with transformation—developing a savings account, covering utilities, and matching his savings so he could break the cycle. Done by brothers and sisters in love, this led to a sense of community, empowerment, and dignity.

6. A quick note on critical theory. Critical theory emerged with the Frank-
furt School in the 1930s but has evolved into nuanced forms since then.
The core concern of critical theory is hegemonic power and the way that
power is hoarded and wielded by groups in positions of dominance.
Individual identity is found in group identity, both in dominant groups
and in oppressed groups. Dominant groups establish society's norms
and then penalize violations of those through multiple forms of cultural
power. Identifying, challenging, and deconstructing these norms and
power structures is the chief duty of a just society. Much of critical
theory is adapted from neo-Marxism, one of the chief competitors in
this generation for the dominant worldview. Though helpful as a diag-
nostic tool with some keen insights, critical theory fails as a worldview or
gospel for followers of Jesus. However, the rise of critical theory should
make us pause and ask ourselves where we have overlooked important
justice issues in our world and how they can be addressed through a
biblical vision of justice and the pursuit of God's kingdom. Our current
moment is an opportunity to preach and live radical discipleship and the
redirection of our privilege, not a moment to be defensive or dismissing.

7. Meaning I believe in equality of opportunity, not equality of outcome.
One involves a concern for what looks like justice and compassion; the
other involves coercive social controls.

8. Lexico, s.v. "Game Theory," www.lexico.com/en/definition/game_theory.

9. N. T. Wright, "Women's Service in the Church," NTWrightPage,
September 4, 2004, http://ntwrightpage.com/2016/07/12/womens
-service-in-the-church-the-biblical-basis.

10. Chris Arnade, "Back Row America," *First Things,* June 2019, www
.firstthings.com/article/2019/06/back-row-america.

11. Nicholas Kristof, "Evangelicals a Liberal Can Love," *New York Times,*
February 3, 2008, www.nytimes.com/2008/02/03/opinion/03kristof
.html.

12. Andy Crouch, *Strong and Weak: Embracing a Life of Love, Risk & True Flourishing* (Downers Grove, IL: InterVarsity, 2016), 151.

Chapter 9: Celebration Must Resist Cynicism

1. Anand Giridharadas, *Winners Take All: The Elite Charade of Changing the World* (New York: Knopf, 2018), 3.

2. John Ortberg, *The Life You've Always Wanted: Spiritual Disciplines for Ordinary People* (Grand Rapids, MI: Zondervan, 2002), 63.

3. James G. Friesen et al., *Living from the Heart Jesus Gave You* (East Peoria, IL: Shepherd's House, 2013), 28.

4. Blaise Pascal, "Pascal's Memorial," in *Greater Shorter Works of Pascal,* trans. Emile Cailliet and John C. Blankenagel (Westport, CT: Greenwood, 1948), 117. The King James pronouns and verb endings have been changed for a more modern reading.

5. Richard J. Foster, *Celebration of Discipline: The Path to Spiritual Growth,* 2nd ed. (New York: Harper & Row, 1988), 195.

6. Rick Howe, *Path of Life: Finding the Joy You've Always Longed For,* rev. ed. (Boulder, CO: University Ministries, 2017), 36.

Epilogue

1. Dietrich Bonhoeffer, *Barcelona, Berlin, New York: 1928–1931,* ed. Clifford J. Green, trans. Douglas W. Stott, vol. 10 of *Dietrich Bonhoeffer Works,* ed. Victoria J. Barnett and Barbara Wojhoski (Minneapolis: Augsburg Fortress, 2008), 313–14.

2. Bonhoeffer, *Barcelona, Berlin, New York,* 317.

3. Dietrich Bonhoeffer, quoted in Eric Metaxas, *Bonhoeffer: Pastor, Martyr, Prophet, Spy* (Nashville: Thomas Nelson, 2010), 113.

4. Bonhoeffer, quoted in Metaxas, *Bonhoeffer,* 107.

5. Metaxas, *Bonhoeffer,* 108.

6. Bonhoeffer, *Barcelona, Berlin, New York,* 315.

7. Dietrich Bonhoeffer, *Conspiracy and Imprisonment: 1940–1945,* ed. Mark S. Brocker, trans. Lisa E. Dahill, vol. 16 of *Dietrich Bonhoeffer Works,* ed. Victoria J. Barnett, Wayne Whitson Floyd Jr., and Barbara Wojhoski (Minneapolis: Augsburg Fortress, 2006), 1.

8. Dietrich Bonhoeffer, *Letters and Papers from Prison,* ed. Eberhard Bethge, enlarged ed. (New York: Touchstone, 1997), 347–48.

Study Guide

1. Bruce Ellis Benson, *Graven Ideologies: Nietzsche, Derrida & Marion on Modern Idolatry* (Downers Grove, IL: InterVarsity, 2002), 19.

2. Peter Scazzero, *Emotionally Healthy Spirituality: It's Impossible to Be Spiritually Mature While Remaining Emotionally Immature,* rev. ed. (Grand Rapids, MI: Zondervan, 2017), 150.

3. Matitiahu Tsevat, quoted in Marva J. Dawn, *Keeping the Sabbath Wholly: Ceasing, Resting, Embracing, Feasting* (1989; repr., Grand Rapids, MI: Eerdmans, 2002), 57.

4. John Ortberg, *The Life You've Always Wanted: Spiritual Disciplines for Ordinary People* (Grand Rapids, MI: Zondervan, 2002), 77.

5. Dietrich Bonhoeffer, *The Cost of Discipleship,* trans. R. H. Fuller (1937; repr., London: SCM Press, 2015), 115.

6. Tim Chester, *A Meal with Jesus: Discovering Grace, Community, and Mission Around the Table* (Wheaton, IL: Crossway, 2011), 12.

7. Arthur C. Brooks, "The Thrill of Political Hating," *New York Times,* June 8, 2015, www.nytimes.com/2015/06/08/opinion/the-thrill-of -political-hating.html.

8. Augustine, *Our Lord's Sermon on the Mount,* ed. D. S. Schaff, trans. William Findlay, in Philip Schaff, ed., *Nicene and Post-Nicene Fathers: First Series* (1888; repr., New York: Cosimo, 2007), 6:26.

9. Preston Sprinkle, "Love Your . . . Enemies? Grace, Nonviolence, Pacifism," PrestonSprinkle.com, www.prestonsprinkle.com/blog/2016/8 /31/love-yourenemies.

10. Andy Crouch, *Strong and Weak: Embracing a Life of Love, Risk & True Flourishing* (Downers Grove, IL: InterVarsity, 2016), 151.

11. "What Is Privilege?," National Conference for Community and Justice, https://nccj.org/what-privilege.

12. Ortberg, *Life You've Always Wanted*, 66.

13. Richard J. Foster, *Celebration of Discipline: The Path to Spiritual Growth*, 2nd ed. (New York: Harper & Row, 1988), 193.